THIS IS THE
LIFE!

THIS IS THE
LIFE!

ENJOYING THE
BLESSINGS AND PRIVILEGES
OF FAITH IN CHRIST

WARREN W. WIERSBE

BakerBooks

a division of Baker Publishing Group
Grand Rapids, Michigan

© 2014 by ScripTex, Inc.

Published by Baker Books
a division of Baker Publishing Group
P.O. Box 6287, Grand Rapids, MI 49516-6287
www.bakerbooks.com

Printed in the United States of America

Library of Congress Cataloging-in-Publication Data
Wiersbe, Warren W.
This is the life! : enjoying the blessings and privileges of faith in Christ /
Warren W. Wiersbe.
    pages cm
    ISBN 978-0-8010-1651-6 (pbk.)
    1. Christian life. I. Title.
BV4501.3.W542155 2014
248.4—dc23   2014018025

15   16   17   18   19   20   21   8   7   6   5   4   3   2

Contents

Preface

"What Is Your Life . . . ?" (James 4:14)

One of my favorite magazine cartoons shows two cows in a pasture, looking over the fence at the traffic going by on the highway. A milk truck is passing, displaying these words on the side panel: "Johnson's Milk—Pasteurized—Homogenized—Vitamins C and D Added." One cow says to the other one, "Sort of makes you feel inadequate, doesn't it?" After hearing many negative sermons and reading many critical book chapters and magazine articles, I get that same bovine feeling, and I wonder why somebody doesn't start accentuating the positive and telling God's people what a great and wonderful life we have as Christians.

But not everybody has a positive view of life. Jewish writer Shalom Aleichem (who gave us Tevye the milkman in *Fiddler on the Roof*) said that life was "a blister on top of a tumor, and a boil on top of that." James M. Barrie, who wrote *Peter Pan*, said that life was "a long lesson in humility," and American poet Carl Sandburg compared life to an onion: "You peel it off one layer at a time, and sometimes you weep." Famous trial lawyer Clarence

Darrow called life "a span of time in which the first half is ruined by our parents and the second half by our children."

The Bible doesn't deny that life has its battles and burdens as well as its blessings. Some of the writers of Scripture see life as a refiner's furnace (Job 23:10), a violent storm (Ps. 42:7), a battle (2 Tim. 2:3), or a difficult race to run (Jer. 12:5). Not only do these writers tell us that life is difficult but they also warn us that life is brief and fragile. When the Lord gave Adam life, He "breathed into his nostrils the breath of life" (Gen. 2:7), and breath has always been associated with brevity and weakness. "Everyone is but a breath," wrote David, "even those who seem secure" (Ps. 39:5 NIV). "What is your life?" asked James. "You are a mist that appears for a little while and then vanishes" (4:14 NRSV). Human life began with a breath, it continues with our breathing, and will end in a moment when we breathe our last. Abraham, Isaac, and Jacob were important and powerful people, but all three "breathed their last" (Gen. 25:8; 35:29; 49:33) and it may be our turn sooner than we expect.

Difficult circumstances we can't always control also contribute to the problems and demands of life, and from ancient days, people have complained about "the times." David lamented in Psalm 11 that all the foundations of life had been destroyed (v. 3) and in Psalm 12 that faithful men and women had vanished from the earth (vv. 1–2). On March 23, 1783, British writer Samuel Johnson said to his friend James Boswell, "I have lived to see things all as bad as they can be." About that same time, Thomas Jefferson wrote in his *Notes on the State of Virginia*, "Indeed, I tremble for my country when I reflect that God is just." Playwright George Bernard Shaw complained, "If the other planets are inhabited, they're using earth as their insane asylum."

~~~

So much for the depressing outlooks on life. The heart of every problem is the problem in the heart, and only our Lord can change the human heart. This book is about the kind of life God wants to give us and how we can receive it through His grace and power. The habits that bind us, the negative attitudes that depress us, the people who bother us, the needs that worry us, and the challenges that frighten us can all be creatively handled by the Lord if we will let Him have His way.

Read and digest the first chapter and be sure of your relationship with the Lord. Then read the table of contents and decide which chapter or chapters best describe your current situation. Start reading there. Each of the chapters is a complete unit, so the choices are yours. Please don't speed-read the chapters but instead read them as if you and I were privately and calmly discussing each one with open Bibles before us. Take time to ponder and pray, and give the Lord opportunity to teach (or remind) you of what you need to know at this time. When I cite Scripture verses that I don't quote, please keep your Bible handy to look up each reference and read it carefully.

Finally, ask the Lord to help you put into practice the principles you are learning. Our obedience turns words into works, and that's the best way to experience spiritual growth. Learning that ignores real living produces a big head but a cold heart and a weak will. Paul warns us that "knowledge puffs up while love builds up" (1 Cor. 8:1 NIV).

"Your words were found, and I ate them, and Your word was to me the joy and rejoicing of my heart, for I am called by Your name, O Lord God of hosts" (Jer. 15:16).

Warren W. Wiersbe

1

Eternal Life

> There was a man of the Pharisees named Nicodemus, a ruler of the Jews. This man came to Jesus by night and said to Him, "Rabbi, we know that You are a teacher come from God; for no one can do these signs that You do unless God is with him." Jesus answered and said to him, "Most assuredly, I say to you, unless one is born again, he cannot see the kingdom of God."
>
> John 3:1–3

Read John 3:1–21. Nicodemus was a member of the Jewish ruling council. Jesus called him Israel's teacher (v. 10), so he must have had a good knowledge of the Scriptures. He appears to be a wealthy man as well as a religious man. Born a Jew, he was a member of the only nation God ever called His chosen people and His "special treasure" (Deut. 7:6). He sought to know the truth and from his heart wanted to love and obey the God of Abraham, Isaac, and Jacob. Nicodemus was a man of character and courage, and yet he knew that something was lacking in his life. He went to get help from Jesus, and the Master told him what was missing: "You must be born again" (John 3:7 NIV). Nicodemus didn't know there was such a thing as a "new birth" and a new beginning in life. The physical blessings we now enjoy came with our physical birth, and if we want spiritual blessings we must experience a spiritual birth. We must receive eternal life.

Eternal Life Is the Very Life of God

The Father, the Son, and the Holy Spirit are eternal; they have neither beginning nor ending. Moses said to the Lord that He was "from everlasting to everlasting" (Ps. 90:2). Moses also called the Lord "the eternal God" (Deut. 33:27), and the prophet Isaiah called God "the High and Lofty One who inhabits eternity" (57:15). Paul addressed the Lord as "the King eternal" (1 Tim. 1:17). The life I have was imparted to me by my parents, but God has "life in Himself" (John 5:26) and that life is imparted to all who repent of their sins and trust Jesus Christ as Savior and Lord (John 10:27–28; Rom. 6:23).

From day to day and season to season, we are accustomed to seeing things and people around us come to an end, either suddenly or gradually, and we are overwhelmed by the very thoughts of eternity and living forever. In his book *The Knowledge of the Holy*, A. W. Tozer said of God's eternality that "our hearts approve with gladness what our reason cannot fully comprehend."[1] That anyone or anything should exist with neither beginning nor ending is something our limited minds cannot grasp. Eternity is "time out of mind," and when the Lord created the first humans, He "put eternity in their hearts" (Eccl. 3:11). This explains why people like us, created in the image of God, have always craved something beyond the mundane things life offers us. Before we met Jesus, we often said to ourselves, "There must be something

1. A. W. Tozer, *The Knowledge of the Holy* (New York: Harper & Row, 1961), 44.

better!" Augustine was right when he wrote, "You have made us for Yourself, and our hearts are restless until they rest in You."

Eternal Life Is the Gift of God

The apostle John wrote of Jesus, "In Him was life, and the life was the light of men" (John 1:4). Jesus conquered death and darkness when on the cross He gave His life as a ransom for sin. "Behold! The Lamb of God who takes away the sin of the world!" shouted John the Baptist (v. 29). "I am the good shepherd," said Jesus. "The good shepherd gives His life for the sheep" (10:11). Throughout Israel's history the sheep had died for the shepherds, but when Jesus came, the Shepherd died for the sheep! "For God so loved the world that He gave His only begotten Son, that whoever believes in Him should not perish but have everlasting life" (3:16). That familiar verse is one of the first we memorized as children in Sunday School, but we had very little understanding of what it meant. It was just words. When a new father or mother holds their first child in their arms, then they begin to understand the Father's love for Jesus *and for us*! According to John 17:23, the Father loves each of His children as much as He loves His own Son!

That Jesus would give His life for us and then, when we trusted Him, *give us His life*, is beyond comprehension. The apostle Paul summarized this miracle in four words: "Christ lives in me" (Gal. 2:20). When the Holy Spirit enters our inner being and takes control, everything changes! "Therefore, if anyone is in Christ, he is a new creation; old things have passed away; behold, all things have become new" (2 Cor. 5:17). Your body becomes the temple of the Holy Spirit and the members of your body the tools the Spirit will use as He empowers you to serve the Lord and glorify Him (1 Cor. 6:19–20). You have a whole new outlook on life as well as a new set of values, and a new desire to serve God and others. The indwelling Spirit enables us to become more and more like Jesus in our thinking (Phil. 2:5) and in our living (Gal. 2:20), and we experience days of heaven on earth because the life of heaven dwells within.

Eternal Life Empowers Us to Do the Will of God and Serve Him

Athletic skill ran in our family—until I came along, and then it ran out. When I was in grade school, I was the last boy chosen for every team. The team captains would argue and the loser would have to take me. When I got to middle school, I was usually on the sidelines, guarding the coats, books, and other possessions of the students playing on the field. I can recall times when I would be up to bat, wishing that Babe Ruth (this was a long time ago!) would enter my body and help me hit a home run. Little did I realize that Someone greater than Babe Ruth—the Holy Spirit of God—would take up residence in my body when I put my faith in Christ one evening at a Youth for Christ rally, and that He would endow me with all that I needed for living the Christian life. "His divine power has given to us all things that pertain to life and godliness" (2 Pet. 1:3).

As I studied my Bible, read Christian books, and listened carefully to preaching and teaching, I began to understand that when the Holy Spirit came into my body, He baptized me into the body of Christ and gave me the spiritual gifts I needed for Christian living and service (1 Cor. 12:1–13). Then I discovered that there was also a filling of the Spirit. Baptism occurs only once but this filling is a repeated experience as we yield to the Lord. I knew that I had to adjust my internal life (thoughts, motives, imaginations, and so forth) to match my eternal life or I would be sinning against the Holy Spirit by lying to the Spirit (Acts 5:1–11), grieving the Spirit (Eph. 4:25–32), and quenching the Spirit (1 Thess. 5:19). It was encouraging and exciting to learn that I was never without divine help as long as I was "walking in the Spirit" and "living in the Spirit" (Gal. 5:16–26). I didn't need Babe Ruth!

You and I may confidently rest on the words Jesus said to His disciples: "And I will pray the Father, and He will give you another Helper, that He may abide with you forever" (John 14:16). In the original Greek text, the word translated *another* means "another of the same kind." He was speaking, of course, about the Holy Spirit of God, and affirming that the Spirit would minister to the disciples just as He had ministered to them. The Spirit is our Helper just as Jesus was the disciples' Helper. In the Old Testament, the Holy Spirit came upon select people and helped them accomplish special tasks; but since Pentecost (Acts 2), the Spirit indwells every believer and helps them in their daily tasks as they serve the Lord. The word translated "Helper" (*paraclete*) means "one called to our side to help us." It has also been translated Comforter, Counselor, and Advocate. Our English word *comfort* comes from the Latin and means "with strength," and the word *advocate* refers to a lawyer who stands beside the accused to give professional help (Mark 13:11). The Holy Spirit does all of this and more for the people of God!

How do we "keep in step" with the Holy Spirit and not forfeit His marvelous ministry? First, we must spend quality time in the Scriptures, which the Holy Spirit wrote, allowing Him to show us Jesus and teach us all that we have in Him. Second, we must seek to glorify Jesus Christ in all that we say and do and with all that we have, for the ministry of the Spirit is not to glorify Himself or us but to glorify Jesus. Our Master said, "He [the Holy Spirit] will glorify Me, for He will take of what is Mine and declare it to you" (John 16:14). I recall hearing Dr. J. Sidlow Baxter preach on this verse and repeatedly say, "Whatever begins with the Holy Spirit will always end at Jesus Christ. He—the Spirit—shall glorify Me—the Savior." If we want our work and walk to glorify Jesus and not ourselves, we must yield to the Spirit and allow Him to have His way. Like the first disciples, we must "give ourselves continually to prayer and to the ministry of the word" (Acts 6:4).

Each of the following chapters describes some aspect of the Christian life that you can experience and enjoy, but unless what I have written in this first chapter is true of your life, the successive chapters will mean very little to you. What Jesus said to Nicodemus, He says to us today: "You must be born again" (John 3:7). The first step in *living* the Christian life is *possessing* eternal life. "For the wages of sin is death, but the gift of God is eternal life in Christ Jesus our Lord" (Rom. 6:23). God's promise is that "whoever calls on the name of the Lord shall be saved" (Acts 2:21).

2

A Trusting Life

Behold the proud, his soul is not upright in him; but the just shall live by his faith.

Habakkuk 2:4

Habakkuk 2:4 is an especially important verse in Scripture because its last seven words are quoted three times in the New Testament: in Romans 1:17, Galatians 3:11, and Hebrews 10:38. The emphasis in Romans is on *the just* and how lost sinners can be justified (declared righteous) before God. The emphasis in Galatians is on *how God's people live*, free from the demands of the Mosaic law and depending wholly on God's grace. The emphasis in Hebrews is on the words *by faith*, a phrase found at least nineteen times in the epistle.

The prophet Habakkuk contrasts two kinds of people in his world and ours: the unbelieving proud and self-sufficient people who think they don't need God, and the saved people who are justified because they have trusted Christ and experienced God's saving grace. The true Christian is saved by faith (Eph. 2:8–9) and lives by faith. "For we walk by faith, not by sight" (2 Cor. 5:7).

What Is Faith?

Cynical American editor H. L. Mencken defined faith as "an illogical belief in the occurrence of the improbable," and humorist Mark Twain had one of his characters say that "faith was believing what you know ain't so." And yet, whether they know it or not, all day long the population of planet Earth lives by faith! They trust their physician's diagnosis and prescription and the pharmacist's skill in compounding the medicine, and yet both of these, being human, could make mistakes. One doctor treated my wife for pneumonia when the pain in her rib cage was actually caused by a damaged ligament. We all make mistakes. Two visits to a therapist cured her. The apostle John wrote, "If we receive the witness of men, the witness of God is greater; for this is the witness of God which He has testified of His Son" (1 John 5:9). If you have ever ridden on an elevator, asked a stranger for directions, eaten food samples in a supermarket, or invested money with a broker, you have acted by faith, for we have no guarantee that what is promised or what we expect will actually happen.

Faith is not a mystical experience of "believing in spite of evidence." That is nothing but superstition and it is foolish. Christian faith is personal confidence in the character of God and in the reliability of His promises as we obey His will. We have plenty of evidence that the Bible is true and that God keeps His promises. Remember, "the witness of God is greater" and always will be. Faith in the Lord enables us to obey Him regardless of the feelings within us, the circumstances around us, or the consequences before us. Abraham believed that God would lead him to the promised land, and He did. When Abraham stopped trusting and started making his own plans, God had to chasten him. *Faith is living without scheming.* Faith is not a special tool we take out of the closet when we face an emergency, because we should "walk by faith" all day long and all life long.

We must learn to trust God in every circumstance and for every need. When my mother-in-law went shopping, she prayed for parking places; when I moved to Chicago with my family, *I* began to pray for parking places! You watch and pray when you drive, you ponder and pray when you shop, you ask God for His help when you go out to minister.

Hebrews 11 describes two kinds of believers, both of whose faith God honored. In verses 1–35, the writer describes those whose faith worked miracles and wrought wonderful victories; but right in the middle of verse 35 he starts describing people who seemed to be failures! The word *others* in verse 35 means "others of a different kind." Both groups had true faith in the Lord, but the second group was different in that it was not granted miraculous deliverance. Instead, they suffered greatly and some of them were slain. Were they people of faith? Yes! Did God give them remarkable deliverance? No! But He did give them the faith to endure persecution and to bring glory to God in their martyrdom (John 21:18–19). The two groups each had the same faith but they did not have the same deliverance; however, both groups brought glory to God.

When I hear well-meaning preachers and teachers declare that God always gives us what we ask in prayer if only we have faith, I shake my head and wonder how many brokenhearted Christians will start questioning God's character and the truth of His promises. Paul was a man of great faith who prayed three times to have his "thorn in the flesh" removed, but God didn't remove it (2 Cor. 12:7–10). Instead, the Lord gave Paul the grace to bear the pain and not complain, which was the blessing he needed. The divine transformation of pain can bring God more glory than the removal of the pain itself; the example of Jesus on the cross proves that. Escaping problems and pains is a wonderful experience—but so is enduring them.

By honestly answering four simple questions, we may test ourselves to see if we are truly praying and walking by faith.

First, *can we back up our prayer requests with Scripture?* "So then faith comes by hearing, and hearing by the word of God" (Rom. 10:17). When I graduated from high school, I had a job waiting for me at a local factory, but I had promised to serve for a week at Vacation Bible School at our church and I couldn't do both. I prayed and asked the Lord to give me something from the Bible that would guide me, and in the course of my daily Bible reading I encountered Matthew 6:33, "But seek first the kingdom of God and His righteousness, and all these things shall be added to you." Claiming this promise, I asked my contact at the factory if I could start a week later, and he gave me permission. Problem solved!

That experience seems trivial when compared with this next one. When my wife and I were serving our first church, it became evident that the congregation would have to build a new sanctuary. My predecessor had wisely built a modest but adequate educational building next to the church building, so we had temporary facilities both for Sunday School classes and church services while building the new sanctuary. My family and close friends know that I am not mechanically inclined and that I have an easier time studying Greek than I do understanding blueprints and specifications. Like Solomon, I was young and inexperienced (1 Chron. 22:5), so I asked the Lord for the promise I needed from the Scriptures.

One morning in my daily reading I came to 1 Chronicles 28:20, where David says to Solomon, "Be strong and of good courage, and do it; do not fear nor be dismayed, for the LORD God—my God—will be with you. He will not leave you nor forsake you, until you have finished all the work for the service of the house of the LORD." What a promise! The Holy Spirit so burned this verse into my heart that it carried me through the entire building program. I had never even built a birdhouse from a kit, yet the Lord gave me and the congregation all that we needed to finish the project.

I am not suggesting you play "Bible roulette" and open the Scriptures just anywhere, close your eyes, and put your finger on a verse. That's not the way of faith. I think it was Campbell Morgan who told about a man who used that approach and his finger landed on Matthew 27:5, "[and Judas] went and hanged himself." So the man tried again, reopened the Bible, and pointed to Luke 10:37, "Go and do likewise." Keep in mind that the Lord gives us these promises not because we find them but *because they find us* in the course of our regular reading of God's Word. Time after time, the Lord has directed me and my wife in that way as we have prayed about important decisions.

Second, *are we doing this for the glory of God?* Abraham is our example. God had told him and his wife that they would have a son in their old age, and they did. "He did not waver at the promise of God through unbelief, but was strengthened in faith, giving glory to God" (Rom. 4:20). God does not answer prayer to please us or to make us rich or famous. He answers prayer to bring glory to His name. In his book *The Tests of Life*, Robert Law wrote, "Prayer is a mighty instrument, not for getting man's will done in Heaven, but for getting God's will done on earth."[1] We must examine our motives as we pray and allow the Spirit to search our hearts. The Lord has answered many prayers for us, but I have lived long enough to be grateful for unanswered selfish prayers.

Third, *do we have peace in our hearts as we pray?* "Now may the God of hope fill you with all joy and peace in believing, that you may abound in hope by the power of the Holy Spirit" (Rom. 15:13). When I was a seminary student, I wanted a part-time job so I consulted the job list on the dormitory bulletin board. One opening seemed to fit my schedule, so I phoned the company, chatted with the HR director, and got the job—over the phone! But once back in my room, I was restless and upset because I knew I had

1. Robert Law, *The Tests of Life: A Study of the First Epistle of St. John*, third ed. (Grand Rapids: Baker, 1982), 304.

THIS IS THE LIFE!

run ahead of the Lord. So I phoned the HR director and apologetically resigned the job, and he was very understanding. A few weeks later, I was invited to become interim pastor of my home church as they searched for a new shepherd, and I stayed with them for seven years! (Usually an interim pastor never gets called, but God had other plans.) No matter what the circumstances are around us, if we have God's peace in our hearts, we can weather the storm and end up at the port of His choosing. The three Hebrew young men are perfect examples of this (Dan. 3).

Fourth, *are we willing to wait?* Serving the Lord involves more than simply doing His bidding. We must do His will in the right way, for the right motive, and at the right time. Romans 10:11 says, "Whoever believes on Him will not be put to shame." This is a quotation from Isaiah 28:16, "whoever believes will not act hastily." When we act impulsively, we usually end up shamefully in trouble, but when we live by faith we are willing to wait on the Lord. David cautions us in Psalm 32:9, "Do not be like the horse or like the mule." Horses are prone to rush ahead and mules often insist on being stubborn. When we walk by faith, we dare not make either of these mistakes or we will be embarrassed and get detoured. Waiting on the Lord is not wasted time; it is invested time as we stay out of God's way until He gives us the signal to act. *God is not in a hurry!* "Wait on the LORD; be of good courage, and He shall strengthen your heart. Wait, I say, on the LORD" (Ps. 27:14). "Rest in the LORD, and wait patiently for Him" (37:7).

Living by faith and trusting the Lord and His promises are not luxuries God gives to the spiritual elite; they are absolute necessities for every child of God. We want the Father to be patient with us as we delay our obedience, but we do not want to be patient with Him as He works out His will in His time! Impatience is usually a mark of either doubt or outright unbelief, while a willingness to wait is evidence of faith. Whenever we become impatient with the Father and get in a hurry, we must remember three "orders" given in the Bible: "Stand still" (Exod. 14:13), "Sit still" (Ruth 3:18), and

"Be still" (Ps. 46:10). If we "stand still," God can go before us and prepare the way, as He did for Israel when they crossed the Red Sea. If we "sit still," God can work for us and accomplish His perfect will, as He did for Ruth. If we will "be still," the Lord will be our refuge and strength in times of trouble, and everything will work out for His glory and our good. The Hebrew word translated "be still" in Psalm 46:10 literally means "take your hands off." How prone we are to try to manage everything ourselves and tell God what to do! Of course, when we know God's will we must be prepared to do it when He gives the signal.

What Does Faith Do for Us?

Faith is the channel that connects us to the treasury of God's grace, from which God can provide all that we need. Through Jesus Christ "we have access by faith into this grace in which we stand" (Rom. 5:2; see Eph. 3:12). In a sermon to his London congregation in 1882, Charles Haddon Spurgeon said, "However, brethren, whether we like it or not, remember, *asking is the rule of the kingdom*." Jesus promised that if we ask in faith, He will graciously give us what we need (Luke 11:9), and James rebukes us when he writes, "Yet you do not have because you do not ask" (James 4:2). The new birth is the first gift God bestows on us when we trust Jesus to save us (Eph. 2:8), and then, as the children of God, for the rest of our lives we may draw upon the "exceeding riches of His grace" (v. 7). "And my God shall supply all your need according to His riches in glory by Christ Jesus" (Phil. 4:19).

Our Father wants us to ask Him to provide what we need for the same reasons fathers and mothers want their children to ask for parental help: asking and receiving are evidences of faith and love. The children confess their own inadequacy and the parents show their generosity. We glorify the Lord when we can say, "Just see what our heavenly Father has done for us!" Believing prayer keeps us in fellowship with God so that He can guide us, teach us, and share His love with us. As children get older, they begin to obey their parents because they love them and want to please them, not because they want "things" for themselves. "But without faith it is impossible to please Him" (Heb. 11:6). We want to be like Jesus and "always do those things that please Him" (John 8:29). That is the kind of witness Paul had: "But as we have been approved by God to be entrusted with the gospel, even so we speak, not as pleasing men, but God who tests our hearts" (1 Thess. 2:4). The people of God who major only in pleasing themselves or satisfying others and not the Lord will not accomplish much for the kingdom of God.

If we live by faith, we have the guarantee of God's guidance day by day and the wisdom we need to make right decisions. "Trust in the LORD with all your heart, and lean not on your own understanding. In all your ways acknowledge Him, and He shall direct your paths" (Prov. 3:5–6). Note that Solomon did not tell us to *ignore* our understanding, because God does instruct a "renewing of your mind" (Rom. 12:2). What He wants is that we not *depend* on our own reasoning. Joshua's defeat at Ai and his covenant with the Gibeonites illustrate the danger of making impetuous decisions (Joshua 7; 9). Joshua blundered because he walked by sight and not by faith, and therefore missed getting God's best. Yes, he was an experienced soldier, but that did not give him the freedom to ignore prayer and seeking God's will.

Faith in the Lord will give us the peace and safety we need in this dangerous world. "The fear of man brings a snare, but whoever trusts in the LORD shall be safe" (Prov. 29:25). On the night of the exodus, Moses did not fear Pharaoh's army behind him or the waters of the Red Sea before him. "Stand still, and see the salvation of the LORD," he instructed the people. "The LORD will fight for you, and you shall hold your peace" (Exod. 14:13–14). God's trusting people are immortal until their work on earth is done. I like the confident attitude of the apostle Paul when he wrote, "But I will tarry in Ephesus until Pentecost. For a great and effective door has opened to me, and there are many adversaries" (1 Cor. 16:8–9). Paul was a realist and did not minimize the obstacles, but he did emphasize the opportunities and the power of God. Ten of the twelve Jewish men who spied out the land of Canaan saw the problems, but Caleb and Joshua saw the opportunities and put their faith in the Lord (Num. 13–14). To walk by faith means to win the battle; to walk by sight can mean to lose the battle and rob the Lord of the glory He deserves.

Like Israel in the wilderness, there are people in our churches who walk by sight and are constantly complaining and repeatedly wanting to "go back to Egypt." Except for Joshua and Caleb, that whole generation of unbelieving Israelites died in the wilderness. Then the Lord took the new generation and gave them victory after victory in Canaan. I fear that too many ministries have been wandering for years in unbelief when they could have been marching in victory. I thank God for my years of service on the Youth for Christ International headquarters staff. We all had plenty of work to do and we had to raise our own support just like missionaries, and the Lord never failed us. We had special days of prayer when we closed down the office (except for the switchboard) and gathered at a local church to spend uninterrupted time in prayer. I remember the all-night prayer meetings at our YFC conventions and the special prayer meetings when an unexpected crisis arose. "And this is the victory that has overcome the world—our faith" (1 John 5:4).

Romans 11:20 tells us we should stand by faith, and 1 Thessalonians 1:3 tells us to work by faith. How could we get any work accomplished if all we did was run around aimlessly? It takes faith to stand and it takes faith to serve. "By faith we understand" (Heb. 11:3), and by faith we see the invisible realities of the kingdom of God (v. 27). Vance Havner used to say, "By faith Moses saw the invisible, chose the imperishable, and did the impossible" (see vv. 23–29). Not a bad record! I thank God for my training in university and seminary and my experience in ministry, but without faith in the Lord these assets would become liabilities.

How Faith Grows

Scripture indicates that, when it comes to faith, there are three possibilities: no faith (Mark 4:40), little faith (Matt. 6:30; 8:26; 14:31; 16:8), and great faith (Matt. 8:10; Luke 7:9). It's interesting that the "great faith" people named were both Gentiles! "Little faith" seemed to be our Lord's favorite nickname for His disciples. Jesus used a little child (Luke 18:17) and a tiny seed (Matt. 17:20) to illustrate the remarkable potential of growth in the spiritual life. Children trust us as they mature and we must never betray that trust or that faith will be damaged. The tiny seed has life in it, and as it is nurtured it will grow to maturity and produce fruit.

The Holy Spirit uses the "word of faith" (Rom. 10:8) to increase our faith because "faith comes by hearing, and hearing by the word of God" (v. 17). Evangelist Dwight L. Moody said, "I used to think I should close my Bible and pray for faith, but I came to see that is was in studying the Word that I was to get faith." I've heard Hebrews 11 called "the Westminster Abbey of Faith," but I question the accuracy of the title. I've visited Westminster Abbey several times and, except for the visitors, everybody in the building is dead! Faith is a living experience! I see Hebrews 11 as "the Hall of Fame of Faith." The people mentioned in that chapter are Olympic champions, bearing witness to us that we can run the race and win in spite of the obstacles.

So, if we want to grow in faith, we must invest time reading and studying the Bible and meditating on what the Lord says. We should compare Scripture with Scripture, memorizing verses and "chewing on them" until they become a part of our inner being. We must "digest" the truth by obeying it so that it becomes a living part of our being. If we do, our faith will grow.

Prayer is another discipline that builds faith. Jesus prayed that Peter's faith would not fail but that he would be restored to service (Luke 22:31–34). As we see the Lord answering prayer in our own lives, we are encouraged to keep on praying and trusting the promises of God. When your prayer life starts to lag, claim Luke 11:9. "And I say to you, ask and it will be given to you; seek, and you will find; knock and it will be opened to you." Our Lord was not just repeating Himself when He spoke those words, because each command carries a special blessing. *Ask* refers to the Father's wealth, *seek* refers to the Father's will, and *knock* refers to the Father's work. (Open doors in Scripture speak of opportunities for service, as in 1 Cor. 16:8–9). We have the right to receive the Father's wealth so long as we are doing the Father's will and are busy in the Father's work, no matter what our calling may be.

By reading Scripture and the biographies and autobiographies of great men and women of faith, I have learned that our Father uses trials and tribulations to increase and perfect our faith. James calls this "the testing of your faith" (James 1:3). *A faith that can't be tested can't be trusted.* I don't know of any servants of God who have been singularly blessed by God and yet have escaped trial and testing and this includes our own beloved Savior. "In the world you will have tribulation," He told the disciples, "but be of good cheer, I have overcome the world" (John 16:33). Unknown to the people they blessed, many of God's choicest servants have lived with personal afflictions and yet continued to serve. During my many years of itinerant ministry, I have been privileged to serve with some of these men and women and have been startled to learn about their "thorns in the flesh"—and they about mine!

I recall a pastor who visited a parishioner in the hospital after she had been through a complex and life-threatening operation. She asked him, "Why did the Lord make me like this?" He quietly replied, "He hasn't made you yet. He is still making you and He is still making me, and He knows what He is doing." She got the point. When you read the Book of Job, you find the patriarch asking many questions of God and of his three friends, and very few of them are really answered. But Job discovered that God's children do not live on explanations; they live on promises. "He knows the way that I take; when He has tested me, I shall come forth as gold"

(Job 23:10). Peter probably had this verse in mind when he wrote, "Beloved, do not think it strange concerning the fiery trial which is to try you, as though some strange thing happened to you; but rejoice to the extent that you partake of Christ's sufferings, that when His glory is revealed, you may also be glad with exceeding joy" (1 Pet. 4:12–13). To be treated the way Jesus was treated certainly is a distinct privilege! Paul called it "the fellowship of His sufferings" (Phil. 3:10).

Joseph experienced hatred and deception at home, lying and physical suffering in Egypt, and separation from the father and brothers he loved. Yet he knew the key to the whole scenario: "God meant it for good" (Gen. 50:20). You would think he had read Romans 8:28!

If we start praying, "Lord, increase our faith" (Luke 17:5), we had better reach for God's Word, go into the prayer closet, and close the door, and when we come out we should expect to experience trials, because that is the only way for God to answer our prayer. Jesus "learned obedience by the things which He suffered" (Heb. 5:8), and so shall we.

"For I consider that the sufferings of this present time are not worthy to be compared with the glory that shall be revealed in us" (Rom. 8:18).

"And this is the victory that has overcome the world—our faith" (1 John 5:4).

3

An Obedient Life

Therefore, my beloved brethren, as you have always obeyed . . . work out your own salvation with fear and trembling, for it is God who works in you both to will and to do of His good pleasure.

Philippians 2:12–13

People who don't learn to obey rarely learn to do anything that is useful and lasting. Those who do not learn to follow orders are rarely chosen to give orders to others. "We learn more by five minutes' obedience than we do by ten years' study," wrote Oswald Chambers, and Jesus agrees. "If anyone wants to do His will, he shall know concerning the doctrine, whether it is from God" (John 7:17). A desire to know and a willingness to obey are the first essentials for learning God's truth and knowing God's will. There is no substitute for obedience, as disobedient King Saul learned from the prophet Samuel. "Has the Lord as great delight in burnt offerings and sacrifices, as in obeying the voice of the Lord?" asked Samuel. "Behold, to obey is better than sacrifice, and to heed as the fat of rams" (1 Sam. 15:22). When he turned his back on the will of God, Saul lost his crown and his life. "Hold fast what you have, that no one may take your crown" (Rev. 3:11).

God has built certain basic laws into His universe. If we obey them, they will work with us and for us and give us success; if we disobey them, they will work against us and possibly destroy us. Whether it's the chemist in the laboratory, the surgeon in the operating room, or the astronaut in the spacecraft, obeying the basic laws is the secret of success. In the Christian life, there is the right way (the will of God) and the wrong way (our own will), and we must make the choice. As C. S. Lewis reminds us, at the judgment, our destiny is determined by whether in life we said to the Lord "Thy will be done," or "My will be done."

Two Essentials: Divine Sovereignty and Human Responsibility

From the creation record in Genesis 1 to the description of the new heavens and earth in Revelation 21–22, our God is presented as the sovereign Lord of all. By calling the Lord "sovereign" we place Him high above everything and give Him complete control over all. The person who wrote Psalm 115 ridiculed idolatry and extolled the indescribable greatness of the God we worship. "Our God is in heaven," he wrote. "He does whatever He pleases" (v. 3). Our God is all-knowing, all-powerful, everywhere-present, and completely free to do His own will without consulting anyone or asking for approval. He is "the King eternal, immortal, invisible . . . God who alone is wise" (1 Tim. 1:17).

It's important to realize that the Lord is free to do as He pleases in heaven, on earth, and under the earth. He created us after His own image, which means we have the ability to think, feel, decide, and act. When the Lord put our first parents into Eden, He told them what to do and what not to do, and left them to their employment and enjoyment. Our God is so great that He could allow them to make a choice. If they made a wrong choice, they would suffer the consequences, but God could still fulfill His great purposes. If we had not been given human responsibility, we would be robots. By giving us this freedom of choice, the Lord enables us to learn by experience, to grow in knowledge, character, and ability, and to love and obey Him because we want to, not because we have to. (I will have more to say about this freedom in chapter 14.)

God created the heavens and the earth without our help, but He ordained that men and women should participate with Him in caring for the earth and accomplishing His good purposes in the world. Adam and Eve worked in the garden. Their son Cain was a farmer and his brother Abel was a shepherd. The sovereignty of God and the responsibility of man worked together for the glory of God and the benefit of mankind. For "it is God who works in you both to will and to do for His good pleasure" (Phil. 2:13). It pleases the Lord greatly when His children freely and lovingly obey Him. "I delight to do Your will, O my God, and Your law is within my heart" (Ps. 40:8).

Two Men: Adam and Jesus

The key passage here is Romans 5:12–21, where Paul contrasts the first Adam, whose disobedience plunged the human race into sin, and the last Adam, Jesus Christ (1 Cor. 15:45), whose obedience brought salvation to the lost world. As you read the text, you get acquainted with four kings: sin is reigning (Rom. 5:21) and therefore death is reigning (vv. 14, 17), because "the wages of sin is death" (6:23), and because God's grace is reigning through Christ (5:21), all who have trusted Christ may "reign in life" through the One, Jesus Christ (v. 17). Are you reigning?

In confirmation class I learned that Jesus was the Prophet when here on earth, and when He returned to heaven He became the

Priest. One day He will come again and will reign as King. But then I discovered that *Jesus Christ is both King and Priest today!* According to Hebrews 6:20, He is "High Priest forever according to the order of Melchizedek." (You'll find this exciting truth explained in Hebrews 7–8.) The children of God have the Holy Spirit interceding within them (Rom. 8:26–27) and the Lord Jesus interceding for them in heaven (Heb. 7:25). Genesis 14:18–24 explains that Melchizedek was both a king and a priest. His name means "king of righteousness" and he was king of Salem, which means "peace." The offices of king and priest and the blessings of righteousness and peace were united in this unique man just as they are in Christ, who is our King and Priest and our righteousness and peace (Ps. 85:10; Isa. 32:17–18; Rom. 5:1). The first Adam disobeyed God and brought sin, conflict, and death into the world, but Jesus Christ "became obedient to the point of death, even the death of the cross" (Phil. 2:8) and brought the righteousness and peace of salvation into the world.

Let's think about Jesus the King. He came to earth and boldly confronted the enemy. He met Satan personally in the wilderness and defeated him in each proposition he offered (Matt. 4:1–11). Because He is victorious, Jesus can help us defeat the evil one when he tempts us. Throughout His three years of ministry, Jesus exposed Satan's lies; delivered Satan's people from disease, bondage, handicaps, and even death; and on the cross defeated him once and for all (John 12:31–32; Col. 2:15). Through His death, resurrection, and ascension, Jesus declares Himself victor and we are "more than conquerors through Him who loved us" (Rom. 8:37). Our King is enthroned in heaven and we are identified with Him in His victories (Eph. 2:4–10). Herod's soldiers mocked our Lord's kingship by dressing Him in a cast-off robe and placing a reed scepter in His hand and a crown of thorns on His head (Matt. 27:27–31). But in heaven today, that mockery has been transformed into majesty! Jesus Christ is Lord and is robed in glory, crowned with glory, and holds "a scepter of righteousness" (Ps. 45:6). He is "the faithful witness, the firstborn from the dead, and the ruler over the kings of the earth . . . and He has made us kings and priests to His God and Father" (Rev. 1:5–6). What a privilege that "as He is [King and Priest], so are we in this world" (1 John 4:17).

The first Adam became a thief, took the fruit of the forbidden tree, ate it, and was cast out of paradise. But Jesus Christ, the last Adam, hanging on the appointed tree, turned to a thief and said, "Assuredly, I say to you, today you will be with Me in Paradise" (Luke 23:43). Hallelujah, what a Savior!

Two Wills

On the battlefield of the Christian life, it's the Father vs. the world (1 John 2:15–17), the Son vs. the devil (John 12:31–33), and the Holy Spirit vs. the flesh, our fallen nature inherited from Adam (Gal. 5:16–26). The basic issue is the will of God: Are we going to be obedient children of God or join the enemy and disobey? The world says, "If the Father really loved you, He would allow you to enjoy worldly things!" The devil says, "God made you with certain desires, so why ignore them? After all, you *are* human!" The flesh declares war on the Holy Spirit and wants us to produce fleshly works, not spiritual fruit.

Most Christians don't suddenly dive into worldliness; instead, they gradually drift back into the old lifestyle and sometimes don't even know what's happening. They first get friendly with the world (James 4:4) and then little by little begin to be "spotted" (defiled) here and there by the world (1:27). If they don't repent and return to the Lord, they start loving the world (1 John 2:15) and becoming conformed to the world (Rom. 12:2). Compromisers don't take seriously God's words of warning in Scripture or His chastening (Heb. 12:1–11), and the day comes when they find themselves condemned with the world (1 Cor. 11:32). Scripture records the tragic endings of believers who were "saved, yet so as through fire" (1 Cor. 3:13–15). Lot and his family come to mind (Gen. 13:11–13; 19:1–29; 2 Pet. 2:7–8), and so does the family of Korah (Num. 16), along with Samson (Judg. 13–15), Ananias and Sapphira (Acts 5), and Demas (2 Tim. 4:10). During my years of ministry, I have grieved over more than one believer who once had a vibrant testimony but slowly drifted back into the old life, and I pray daily for myself, "Lord, help me to end well."

Cultivating a negative attitude toward the will of God is the first step toward disappointment and defeat. God's will is not chains (Ps. 2:3) but cords of love (Hos. 11:4). His will is not a bit and bridle (Ps. 32:8–9) but the secret of joyful freedom. "And I will walk at liberty, for I seek your precepts" (119:45). God wants us to *know* His will (Acts 22:14), *obey* His will from the heart (Eph. 6:6), *understand* His will (5:17), and *delight* in His will (Ps. 40:8). God's will is not a buffet dinner where we choose only what pleases us. His will is a rich and nutritious meal prepared especially for us, and we must accept all of it. "My food is to do the will of Him who sent Me and to finish His work," said Jesus (John 4:34). God's will is not punishment but nourishment. *The will of God is the expression of the love of God to each of His children, the invitation to a rich and fruitful life.* "The counsel of the LORD stands forever, the plans of His heart to all generations" (Ps. 33:11). His will comes from His heart.

God's plans for us were made by the Lord long before we were ever conceived or born (Ps. 139:13–16; Jer. 1:5). In His love, the Lord has equipped us with just the tools we need to serve Him. Furthermore, the Lord has already prepared the works He wants us to do! "For we are His workmanship, created in Christ Jesus for good works, which God prepared beforehand that we should walk in them" (Eph. 2:10). My prayer is that I might one day be able to stand before the Father and say what Jesus said in His great high priestly prayer: "I have glorified You on the earth. I have finished the work which You have given Me to do" (John 17:4). Our lives are not accidents but divine appointments, and if we are obedient to the Lord, He will see to it that we fulfill the ministry He has assigned us to do (2 Tim. 4:7–8).

Our obedience should be motivated by our love for the Lord (John 14:15, 21; 15:10, 14), balanced by our reverence and fear of the Lord. "You shall walk after the LORD your God and fear Him, and keep His commandments and obey His voice; you shall serve Him and hold fast to Him" (Deut. 13:4). We Christians tell the lost that God will judge them one day, and this statement is true, *but the Lord also judges His people if they willfully disobey Him!* Psalm 50:4 declares, "He shall call to the heavens from above, and to the earth, that He may judge His people." The verse is quoted in Hebrews 10:30 and applied to believers today. There is joy in serving Jesus, but we should also heed Psalm 2:11: "Serve the LORD with fear, and rejoice with trembling."

"If anyone wills to do His will," said Jesus, "he shall know concerning the doctrine" (John 7:17). British Greek scholar Henry Alford translates this verse, "If any man be willing to do His will, he shall know concerning the teaching." *A willingness to obey the Father is the first requirement for knowing and doing the will of God.* God doesn't reveal His will to us to get our approval, but to command our obedience.

Two Nations

The only ancient nation whose history we have from start to finish is the nation of Israel, and it's the only nation on earth today with whom God has made a covenant. Patriotic Americans like to think that the United States is a "covenant nation" because of its Christian forbearers, but that isn't true. The only other "covenant nation" in today's world is the church, for the Lord has made a "new covenant" with His believing people (Matt. 26:26–29). Jesus makes this clear in Matthew 21:43, "Therefore I say to you, the kingdom of God will be taken from you [Israel] and given to a nation bearing the fruits of it [the church]." Peter wrote to the believers of his day, "But you are a chosen generation, a royal priesthood, a holy nation, His own special people" (1 Pet. 2:9). The church is a "holy nation" called to reach the nations with the gospel.

The Lord set Israel apart to accomplish specific purposes: bearing witness to the one true and living God, bringing the promised Savior into the world ("salvation is of the Jews," John 4:22), forming the nucleus of the first church, and writing the holy Scriptures. The Lord has set apart the church as a holy nation to reach the nations. Israel failed to obey God and instead imitated the wicked nations around them, and therefore they lost God's blessing. The church today must not conform to this world (Rom. 12:2) but declare and demonstrate the gospel of Jesus Christ. If we obey the Lord, He will use us to reach others; if we compromise with the world, He cannot answer our prayers or bless our service.

Our citizenship is in heaven (Phil. 3:20), our names are written down in heaven (Luke 10:20), and we are "pilgrims" in this world (1 Pet. 1:1). A fugitive is running from home, a vagabond has no home, a stranger is away from home, but a pilgrim is heading home. This dual citizenship forces us to look at this world from the viewpoint of heaven. "If then you were raised with Christ, seek those things which are above, where Christ is, sitting at the right hand of God. Set your mind on things above, not on things on the earth" (Col. 3:1–2). When we start to look at the things of Christ from the world's point of view, we have taken the first step away from the blessings God wants to give us.

The citizen of a country speaks the language of that country, obeys the laws of that country, and seeks to enhance the glory of that country. As citizens of heaven, we aren't ashamed to speak heaven's truth, obey heaven's laws, defend heaven's reputation, and do everything we can to bring glory to the triune God who reigns in heaven.

Therefore, my beloved, as you have always obeyed, not as in my presence only, but now much more in my absence, work out your own salvation with fear and trembling; for it is God who works in you both to will and to do for His good pleasure. (Phil. 2:12–13)

We obey God and work for Him because He graciously works in us and through us to accomplish His will. To be obedient to the will of God is not an accident or an insignificant incident but a divine appointment that, if kept, leads to achievement to the glory of God.

"Your will be done on earth as it is in heaven" (Matt. 6:10).

"Then I said, 'Here am I! Send me'" (Isa. 6:8).

4

A Victorious Life

Finally, my brethren, be strong in the Lord and in the power of His might. Put on the whole armor of God, that you may be able to stand against the wiles of the devil.

Ephesians 6:10–11

No sooner had the obedient Son of God been baptized in the Jordan River by John the Baptist, commended from heaven by the Father, and empowered by the Holy Spirit than He was led into the wilderness to do battle against Satan (Matt. 4:1–11). That conflict continued during the years of His public ministry and was climaxed in Christ's victory by His death, resurrection, and ascension. Christ is the conqueror and is enthroned today in glory. We should rejoice that Jesus is "far above all principality and power and might and dominion" (Eph. 1:21), and we should accept His invitation to share in His victory. Satan today is at war with the church of Jesus Christ and he knows that his time is short (Rev. 12:12).

However, many professed Christians today are living as though they were on a playground, not a battleground. They forget (or perhaps never knew) that Jesus warned His disciples, "In the world you will have tribulation" (John 16:33), and the apostle Paul wrote that "all who desire to live godly in Christ Jesus will suffer persecution" (2 Tim. 3:12). Jesus was lied about, ridiculed, threatened, beaten, and crucified *by the governmental and religious leaders of His day*, and Paul wrote that every true believer would share in "the fellowship of His sufferings" (Phil. 3:10). In his Gospel, the apostle John vividly describes our Lord's conflicts and then he applies them to the church in his first epistle. Finally, he dramatically portrays this awesome conflict in the Book of Revelation—Christ vs. Antichrist, the new Jerusalem vs. Babylon, the Lamb of God vs. the beast from hell.

Yes, God will one day judge this world, but first, judgment begins "at the house of God" (1 Pet. 4:17). In His letters to the seven churches (Rev. 2–3), Jesus calls His people to be overcomers, but God's household today appears to be overcome and filled with underachievers. To put it bluntly, we are not ready for battle. Too many professed Christians in and out of our evangelical churches are not prepared to face the official persecution that is coming. Peter puts it this way:

> Beloved, do not think it strange concerning the fiery trial which is to try you, as though some strange thing happened to you, but rejoice to the extent that you partake of Christ's sufferings, that when His glory is revealed, you may also be glad with exceeding joy. If you are reproached for the name of Christ, blessed are you, for the Spirit of glory and of God rests upon you. On their part He is blasphemed, but on your part He is glorified. (1 Pet. 4:12–14)

The fiery trial did come in Peter's day, and when it comes again, God's people must be prepared. Peter counsels us to arm ourselves with the same attitude of mind that Jesus had when He faced the enemy and went to the cross (vv. 1–2). Outlook helps to determine outcome, and if our outlook is not biblical and sober our outcome will be tragic.

In this chapter, I want to describe the equipment and enablement of a faithful Christian soldier. I realize that some people resent the military emphasis in Scripture, *but the emphasis is there and we dare not ignore it.* The conflict the church is facing cannot be handled with the kid gloves of sentimental diplomacy. We must wear the whole armor of God and know how to use the equipment the Lord has made available to us (Eph. 6:10–20).

Attention! Here are the orders from the Captain of our salvation (Heb. 2:10)!

Remember That You Are Always a Soldier, Either on Duty or AWOL

It's important to realize that the instant we trusted Jesus Christ as Savior and Lord, we became soldiers in the army of God. We were not asked to volunteer, for the Captain of our salvation has decreed that everyone who belongs to the family of God also belongs to the army of God—whether they obey orders or not. The devil is our enemy and he and his demonic army use the world and the flesh to tempt us to sin. Satan is a liar (serpent) who deceives and a lion who devours (John 8:44; 2 Cor. 11:3; 1 Pet. 5:8–9), and we must take him seriously. To jest about him is to play right into his hands.

Satan is also called Apollyon, which means "destroyer" (Rev. 9:11). In past centuries, he tried to destroy the Jewish nation and prevent the birth of Jesus, and since Pentecost (Acts 2) he has tried to destroy the church and silence its witness. But history has proved that the blood of the martyrs only strengthens and expands the church. Satan is a counterfeiter and his servants pretend to follow Christ but are only masquerading (2 Cor. 11:13–15). His false apostles preach a false gospel (Gal. 1:6–10) that leads people into bondage instead of into the freedom of salvation in Jesus Christ.

This means we must be alert and awake at all times, never off duty. Peter's admonition that we be sober and vigilant (1 Pet. 5:8–9) came from a man who was *not* sober and vigilant, one who denied the Lord and tried to kill a man! We must respect Satan's subtlety and strength and turn to the Lord for help when we know the enemy is at work.

Always Wear Your Armor

Five words in 2 Samuel 11:1 explain why David committed adultery with Bathsheba, plotted the death of her husband, and lied about the whole affair for nearly a year: "But David remained at Jerusalem." *He laid aside his armor!* He should have been with his army, attacking the enemy, but instead he stayed home and was attacked by a far worse enemy *and lost the battle!* Every Christian is commanded to "endure hardship as a good soldier of Jesus Christ" (2 Tim. 2:3) and to "fight the good fight of faith" (1 Tim. 6:12). We can do it successfully if we wear the armor described in Ephesians 6:10–20 and know how to use it. Satan's evil tactics are shrewd (2 Cor. 11:1–4) and the days are evil (Eph. 5:16; 6:13). Note that we need "the whole armor" and not just one or two parts, and that we must stand our ground and withstand our enemy. In Jesus Christ we stand victorious, but Satan wants us to retreat and lose the ground Jesus won for us on the cross. We are fighting from Christ's victory and not for our own victory, for by faith we are already standing on holy ground. Read Joshua 5:13–15 to get the picture. The parts of the armor all relate to the person and work of our Lord Jesus Christ (Rom. 13:12–14; Eph. 4:17–24), so to put on the armor is to put on Christ and abide in Him (Col. 3:8–17).

The girdle of truth (Eph. 6:14). This was not a narrow belt but more like a heavy leather and metal apron. From the waist down to about four inches above the knees, it went around the soldier's body and covered him front and back. It helped to keep the other

41

parts of the armor together, and provided a place where the soldier could carry some of his equipment, such as a short spear, a pouch, and a dagger. The word *truth* here means "integrity," for just as the girdle held the armor together, personal integrity holds our character together and delivers us from hypocrisy and duplicity, what the world calls "talking out of both sides of your mouth." An integer is a whole number and integrity is wholeness. A fraction is a part of a number and corresponds to hypocrisy and duplicity, saying one thing but living quite another. "Behold, You desire truth in the inward parts" (Ps. 51:6). To be double-minded and try to serve two masters is to lose integrity and practice hypocrisy.

The breastplate of righteousness (Eph. 6:14) was made of metal and protected the soldier's torso, front and back. The Christian soldier has two kinds of righteousness: *imputed righteousness*, which is the righteousness of Christ put to our account when we first trusted Him (Rom. 4:13–23; 2 Cor. 5:21), and *imparted righteousness*, which the Holy Spirit builds into our character as we walk by faith and obey the Lord. A theologian would call the first *justification* and the second *sanctification*. Imputed righteousness never changes, for the Father always accepts us in Christ (Eph. 1:1–6), but imparted righteousness does change as we daily walk with the Lord and obey Him. If we wear the breastplate, the accusations and attacks of the devil cannot hurt us. The breastplate protects the heart, for it is out of the heart that life flows (Prov. 4:23).

The shoes of peace (Eph. 6:15) enable the soldiers to stand, walk, run, and keep their balance as they do battle. Roman soldiers wore strong leather sandals with hobnails on the soles and thongs to hold the shoes in place. The Lord wants us to take our stand for Him and the gospel (1 Cor. 15:1, 58) and be able to maneuver and get the best of the enemy. Since we are at peace with God (Rom. 5:1), we can wear shoes of peace and bring peace to others who are fighting battles. The soldier who is at war with himself or with others will not be able to be an instrument of God's peace. Having peace with God through the cross and the peace of God in our hearts (Phil. 4:6–7), we are actually "waging peace" and not fighting a traditional war. This inner peace gives us stability and mobility as we oppose Satan and his hosts. We are not fighting flesh and blood but the Satanic forces that use people to oppose the work of Christ. Christians are to be peacemakers and not troublemakers. If our lives and ministries cause trouble, it's because the world hates us and the gospel.

The shield of faith (Eph. 6:16) protected the soldier and his armor. The Roman shield measured two feet by four feet and was so constructed that a row of soldiers could lock their shields together and form a wall. The enemy would shoot fiery arrows that would strike the shields and be extinguished. Satan shoots at us the fiery darts of fear, confusion, doubt, vicious criticism, false accusations, and outright lies and slander. Jesus was treated that way and so were the apostles. If these darts are not extinguished, the fire will spread and do terrible damage. Satan reminds us of our past sins and mistakes and tries to discourage us, but when we exercise faith in God's promises we win the victory (Rev. 12:7–12). "His faithful promises are your armor and protection" (Ps. 91:4 NLT). "And this is the victory that has overcome the world—our faith" (1 John 5:4).

The helmet of salvation (Eph. 6:17). The Roman soldier's helmet was made of bronze and covered his head and cheeks, not unlike the helmets we see on cyclists today. It isn't enough for a soldier to have a protective shield; he must also protect his head and mind if he is to be an intelligent soldier. It isn't difficult to see the spiritual lessons here. We must beware of the instability of a *divided mind* (James 1:8) and be like Jesus, who set His face to go to Jerusalem to die (Luke 9:51). We cannot serve two masters (Matt. 6:24). We must also beware of a *deceived mind* (2 Cor. 11:3), for Satan is a counterfeiter and makes every attempt to lure us away from the truth. As he did with Eve (Gen. 3), Satan first questions God's Word (v. 1), then denies God's Word (v. 4), and then substitutes his own lie (v. 5). It's dangerous to have a *doubtful mind* (Luke 12:29) that is anxious and worried about the affairs of life. This often leads to a *discouraged mind*. In 1 Thessalonians 5:8, Paul calls the helmet "the hope of salvation," because hope vanishes when we become discouraged and the future becomes dark and dangerous. Daily I must be in the Word of God, allowing the Holy Spirit to transform my mind so that I don't reason as the world does.

The sword of the Spirit (Eph. 6:17) is the soldier's weapon of both offense and defense. Hebrews 4:12 describes this spiritual sword:

> For the word of God is living and powerful, and sharper than any two-edged sword, piercing even to the dividing of soul and spirit, and of the joints and marrow, and is a discerner of the thoughts and intents of the heart.

The Lord uses the sword on unbelievers to convict them of sin and bring them to salvation (Acts 2:37–38), but He also uses it on His own children to impart what is right and remove what is wrong. Unlike a material sword, God's Word never gets dull. It contains its own power and it imparts life instead of death! Our Lord used the Scriptures to defeat the devil in the wilderness (Matt. 4:1–11) and so may we when Satan tempts us today. "Your word have I hidden in my heart that I might not sin against You" (Ps. 119:11).

"Stand Up, Stand Up for Jesus" is a hymn we used to sing in Sunday School and youth meetings. The third verse says, "Put on the gospel armor / Each piece put on with prayer." It is by faith that we put on the armor and it is by faith that we confront the enemy. "Therefore submit to God. Resist the devil, and he will flee from you" (James 4:7).

Report for Duty Daily

"My voice You shall hear in the morning, O LORD; In the morning I will direct it to You, and I will look up" (Ps. 5:3). The word translated *direct* comes out of the Jewish priestly vocabulary and pictures the priest at the altar, arranging the wood and the pieces of the sacrifice. But it also has a military meaning: to deploy troops, to take your stand for the battle. It is used this way in 1 Samuel 17 to describe the giant Goliath "taking his stand" and defying Saul's army. Each morning when I have my quiet time, I am like a priest bringing sacrifices to the Lord and also like a soldier reporting for the duties of the day. When I pray, I give God my burdens, and when I read the Word of God and meditate, He gives me my orders. Our Lord awakened early each morning to spend time alone with His Father before the crowds gathered (Isa. 50:4–6; Mark 1:35), and this is a good example for us to follow. Resist the enemy.

Three times in Ephesians 6 Paul emphasizes that we must take a stand so that we may be able to withstand the evil one. Before the battle, we put on the armor of God that we may be able to stand (vv. 11, 13). Then we take our stand in the strength of the Lord and withstand the enemy. Having won, we continue to take our stand lest the enemy return and catch us unawares (v. 14). Paul warned Timothy that, if he wanted to please his Commander, he had better not get entangled with the world and become a double-minded soldier (2 Tim. 2:4).

It is the power of the Lord that sees us through and not our own strength, wisdom, and ability. Paul commands us to "be strong in the Lord and in the power of His might" (Eph. 6:10). How do we receive this power? By "praying always with all prayer and supplication in the Spirit" (v. 18). After their deliverance from Egypt, the Israelites confronted the Amalekites and defeated them because Moses, Aaron, and Hur were interceding on the mountain while Joshua and his men were wielding their swords down below. We not only put on the armor through prayer but we also use the equipment in battle through prayer.

Note that Paul admonishes us to "be watchful" in our praying (v. 18). We pray with our eyes wide open lest the enemy stage a sneak attack. When Nehemiah and his workers were rebuilding the walls of Jerusalem, their enemies threatened them, so the Jews prayed and set a watch (Neh. 4:7–9). If we do what we can, the Lord will do the rest. Jesus taught His disciples to "watch and pray" (Matt. 26:41; Mark 13:33; 14:38) and so did the apostle Paul in both Ephesians 6:18 and in Colossians 4:2. Devotion and discernment go together.

Be Mindful of Other Believers

Paul closed his epistle (Eph. 6:19–24) by admonishing the Ephesian believers to include him and his helpers in their prayers. Paul was a brilliant man, a godly man who had been to heaven and back, and yet he was humble enough to ask for their prayer support. All true believers are in this battle against Satan, and we need to pray for one another. "Resist him," wrote Peter, "steadfast in the faith, knowing that the same sufferings are experienced by your brotherhood in the world" (1 Pet. 5:9). Have you noticed that the personal pronouns in the Lord's Prayer are plural? It's not "My Father" but "Our Father . . . our daily bread . . . our trespasses" and so on. We are part of a wonderful worldwide family and are obligated to pray for the brothers and sisters whose circumstances we know.

"It is foolish to underestimate the power of Satan, but it is fatal to overestimate it," said missionary Ruth Paxson at the 1936 British Keswick conference. Christ has overcome Satan and will give us the victory if we are wearing the armor and trusting Him.

5

A Joyful Life

Rejoice in the Lord always. Again I will say, rejoice!

Philippians 4:4

Joy is the spontaneous, exultant response of the Christian's heart to the Lord when it is moved by what God is, what God says in His Word, or what God has done or is doing. Happiness is not the same as joy, because happiness depends largely on happenings. Joy can come even in the midst of sorrow. The English word *happen* comes from the old word *hap*, which is connected with *luck* and *chance*, words that people who believe in God's wise and loving providence should avoid. The Lord "gives us richly all things to enjoy" (1 Tim. 6:17), and He can make all things work together for our good and His glory (Rom. 8:28).

If you go searching for joy, you won't find it, because joy is the by-product of abiding in Christ and His Word, obeying Him, and seeking to serve and glorify Him. Jesus used the birth of a baby to illustrate the miracle of Christian joy (John 16:20–22). The mother experiences pain as she delivers her child, but once delivered, *the same baby that caused the pain now brings joy!* It's a miracle of transformation, not substitution. The Lord commands us to be joyful, and if we are not joyful we are disobedient and have nobody to blame but ourselves. There are many spiritual keys to the joyful Christian life and the Holy Spirit helps us to find and use the right one for each situation.

The Joy of Jesus

In a message I gave some years ago at a summer Bible conference, I mentioned that Jesus experienced many joys during His earthly ministry. After the meeting, I was confronted by a feisty elderly lady who accused me of being a heretic. "Jesus was a man of sorrows and acquainted with grief!" she shouted. I tried to show her the passages that mentioned the joys of our Savior, but she refused to read them, turned her back on me, and triumphantly marched away. The Father wants us to become more and more like His Son, and that includes experiencing joy. "But the fruit of the Spirit is love, joy . . ." wrote the apostle Paul in Galatians 5:22. Not to be joyful, even in times of pain and sorrow, is to grieve the Spirit of God.

When the Seventy returned from their ministry journey and told Jesus what had happened, "Jesus rejoiced in the Spirit" and praised His Father for the victories they had won over the devil (Luke 10:17–24). In the upper room, Jesus said, "These things have I spoken to you, that My joy may remain in you and that your joy may be full" (John 15:11). Had Jesus never manifested joy, this statement would have perplexed the disciples. Jesus prayed that His joy might be fulfilled and manifested in His disciples (17:13), and the Father answered that prayer. Yes, Jesus experienced sorrow, pain, and death, but He also experienced joy.

There were several spiritual resources that enabled Jesus to endure the cross, and one of them was "the joy that was set before Him" (Heb. 12:2). What was that joy? Verse 24 of the epistle of

Jude gives the answer: "[He] is able to keep you from stumbling and to present you faultless before the presence of His glory with exceeding joy." Anticipating His future joy with His glorified church in heaven enabled Jesus to endure Calvary's pain and shame. What a joyful occasion it will be when He presents us to His Father! No matter what our trials may be today, the best is yet to come. "Let us be glad and rejoice and give Him glory, for the marriage of the Lamb has come, and His wife has made herself ready" (Rev. 19:7). Looking ahead to the glories of our heavenly home is a sure cure for the sorrows of a troubled heart (John 14:1–3).

The Joy of Believing God

In spite of the fact that Paul was a prisoner in Rome when he wrote to the Philippians, his letter is saturated with joy. When God's children live in God's will, they will experience the joy of the Lord regardless of their circumstances. Paul was especially joyful because of the Philippian believers' "progress and joy of faith" (Phil. 1:25). "I am convinced that I will remain alive so that I can continue to help all of you grow and experience the joy of your faith" (NLT). It is a joyful challenge to live by faith and to grow in faith. We enter God's family when we trust Christ for our salvation, but that's only the beginning. As God's children, we live by promises and not by explanations. Knowing that our Father loves us, plans for us, directs us, cares for us, and gives us the privilege of serving Him, we rest joyfully in His perfect will. It's the joy of faith!

But this joy of faith fills our hearts only when we submit to the Lord, trust Him, and give Him our best. "My heart rejoices in the Lord," sang Hannah after giving her firstborn son to serve in God's tabernacle (1 Sam. 2:1), and when Mary yielded herself to the Lord to bear the Messiah, she sang, "My soul magnifies the Lord, and my spirit has rejoiced in God my Savior" (Luke 1:46–47). When we give ourselves and our sacrifices to the Lord, the song of the

Lord is sure to follow. "When the burnt offering began, the song of the Lord also began" (2 Chron. 29:27).

The joy of believing leads us to the joy of answered prayer. "Ask and you will receive, that your joy may be full," said Jesus (John 16:24). Prayer is energized by faith, and faith is strengthened by the Word of God (Rom. 10:17). There are long prayers of praise and confession in the Bible as well as brief "emergency prayers" such as Peter's "Lord, save me" (Matt. 14:30–31). It isn't the length of our prayers but the strength of our faith that makes the difference. As I review more than six decades of ministry, my heart still leaps for joy as I recall how God has answered prayer—and still does! How grateful I am for those who prayed and taught me to pray! My four years of ministry with Youth for Christ International was like a graduate course in prayer. "According to your faith let it be to you" (9:29).

The Joy of Serving God

If we are serving the right master, in the right way, for the right purpose, and with the right attitude, we will serve joyfully and never think of quitting. For the Christian, Jesus is the right Master, building His church is the right purpose, laboring in faith and love for His glory is the right way to do His work, and joy is the right attitude, because it is a privilege to serve the Lord. There are times when the enemy opposes us, our strength begins to fail, and we feel like quitting; that's when we should rejoice in the Lord and keep right on working. "Serve the LORD with gladness; come before His presence with singing" (Ps. 100:2). "Do not sorrow, for the joy of the LORD is your strength" (Neh. 8:10). God sent the Jews into captivity because they had lost the joy of the Lord and had begun to serve dead idols. "You did not serve the LORD your God with joy and gladness of heart for the abundance of all things" (Deut. 28:47).

A remnant of Jews had returned to their land after the Babylonian captivity and were rebuilding the walls of Jerusalem under the leadership of Nehemiah the governor. The work was not easy and the enemies around the city did all they could to frighten the workers and interrupt the work. Ezra the scribe came to the city and taught the people God's Word, and this encouraged them to keep on working. He pointed out that it was time for them to celebrate the feast of tabernacles (Lev. 23:33–44) and to rejoice at what the Lord had done when He delivered their ancestors from Egypt. Their God had done wonders for them in the past and He would not abandon them now. They should rejoice in the Lord, for "the joy of the Lord is your strength." The people obeyed God's word, celebrated the feast, and "there was very great gladness" (Neh. 8:17).

No matter what tasks the Lord gives us, whether temporary or permanent, there are two things we can expect: the enemy will oppose us and the Lord will give us enough wisdom and strength to complete the work for God's glory. Paul's greatest desire was to finish his race with joy (Acts 20:24)—and he did! "I have fought the good fight, I have finished the race, I have kept the faith" (2 Tim. 4:7). When Jesus came to earth, He came as a servant, and He expects us to be servants. Paul frequently called himself "the bondservant of Jesus Christ."

In one of his essays, Robert Louis Stevenson wrote, "Don't judge each day by the harvest you reap but by the seeds that you plant." We serve a day at a time, and "as your days, so shall your strength be" (Deut. 33:25). We may go out with weeping, but God promises that the seeds we sow will one day produce the harvest (Ps. 126:6; John 4:35–38).

The Joy of Finding the Lost

If Luke's Gospel were a newspaper, chapter fifteen would be the "Lost and Found" column. It tells us about a shepherd who found a lost sheep, a woman who found a lost coin, and a father who welcomed home a lost son. The chapter also emphasizes the joy of the people who recovered what had been lost. The shepherd rejoiced (and the sheep probably did too!), the woman rejoiced, and so did the family, except for the elder brother. Certainly there is joy in our hearts whenever people put their faith in the Savior. Philip found the lost Ethiopian treasurer and led him to Christ, and the man "went on his way rejoicing" (Acts 8:39). Paul and Silas led the Roman jailer and his family to Christ and joy came into their home (16:34). Peter called this "joy inexpressible and full of glory" (1 Pet. 1:8).

Jesus has commissioned His church to declare the good news of salvation to all nations, and our motive should be that of Paul: "For the love of Christ constrains us" (2 Cor. 5:14). The witness of some believers is motivated by guilt ("It's my job!") and others by pride ("I got another one!"), but the only motivation that the Spirit seeks is our love for Christ and for lost sinners. Our Lord came to seek and to save the lost (Luke 19:10), and He is pleased when we are alert to opportunities for witness. If we are yielded to the Spirit, He will guide us and enable us to plant the seed.

The Joy of Worshiping God

Worship is the most important ministry of the individual Christian and of each local assembly of believers, for everything we are and everything we do flows out of worship. Believers who ignore worship are like vehicles without fuel or gardens without sun and water. We may have gifts and abilities that impress people, but if we don't worship God and receive the Spirit's power, we can do nothing (John 15:5; Acts 1:8). The early church waited in prayer for ten days until the Spirit empowered them at Pentecost, and then they gave their public witness to the lost and three thousand people were saved (Acts 1–2).

There is no joy like the joy of worship. "Rejoice in the LORD, O you righteous! For praise from the upright is beautiful. Praise the LORD with the harp; make melody to Him with an instrument of ten strings. Sing to Him a new song; play skillfully with a shout of joy" (Ps. 33:1–3). Worship is God-centered and focuses on His glorious attributes and ministries, His wonderful works, His infallible words, and His precious Son. True worship brings joy to our hearts, and as our hearts express our praise it brings joy to the Lord. A worshiping believer hears the hills and mountain rejoicing (Isa. 55:12), for heaven and earth declare the glory of God. Yes, there are occasions when our worship is solemn, perhaps even silent; but ultimately our tongues must express what our hearts experience. "Enter into His gates with thanksgiving, and into His courts with praise. Be thankful to Him and bless His name" (Ps. 100:4).

I have traveled enough in this world to know that Christians in different cultures express their worship in different ways. The main thing is that our worship come from sincere hearts of love and is controlled by the Scriptures and the Spirit (Eph. 5:18–19; Col. 3:16). If my own daily private worship pleases God, then my sharing in public worship should please Him also. If I am to glorify God in public worship on the Lord's Day, I must be in a "worship mode" every day and all week long. How sad it is that some of God's people attend public worship unprepared. This grieves the Spirit and affects the whole body. We should go "to the house of God, with the voice of joy and praise" (Ps. 42:4). "My lips shall greatly rejoice when I sing to You, and my soul, which You have redeemed" (71:23).

Some Christians like to blame their low spiritual state on what they call "dull worship at church," but often the dullness is not in the worship but in the worshipers! By their own neglect, they "have become dull of hearing" (Heb. 5:11) and can no longer discern the voice of the Spirit in the music, the prayers, the Scripture readings, and the message from the pulpit. I heard about a church member who, after the service, told the pastor, "Your sermon was over my head." Quietly the pastor replied, "Let's ask the Lord to raise your head." God's warning about the dullness of hearing that accompanies undisciplined living is repeated seven times in the Bible! You find it in Isaiah 6:9–10, Matthew 13:14–15, Mark 4:11–12, Luke 8:9–10, John 12:37–41, Acts 28:25–27, and Romans 11:8. Are we getting the message?

The Joy of Being Forgiven and Forgiving Others

David expressed this truth after the Lord had forgiven him for committing adultery, scheming to murder the innocent husband, and covering it all up for nearly a year (2 Sam. 11–12). "Blessed is he whose transgression is forgiven, whose sin is covered. Blessed is the man to whom the LORD does not impute iniquity, and in whose spirit there is no deceit . . . I acknowledged my sin to You . . . and You forgave the iniquity of my sin" (Ps. 32:1–2, 5). "If we confess our sins, He is faithful and just to forgive us our sins and to cleanse us from all unrighteousness. . . . And if anyone sins, we have an Advocate with the Father, Jesus Christ the righteous" (1 John 1:9; 2:1). As our heavenly High Priest, Jesus can keep us from sinning if we come to the throne of grace for help (Heb. 4:14–16). But if we do sin, Jesus our Advocate intercedes for us and gives us forgiveness when we repent and confess.

In the life of a Christian, there are three aspects of forgiveness that must be distinguished, the first of which is *final forgiveness*. We received that when we trusted Jesus to save us. "In Him we have redemption through His blood, the forgiveness of sins, according to the riches of His grace" (Eph. 1:7; see Col. 2:13–14). But after we are saved, we still have the ability to sin, and if we do it breaks our communion with the Lord and we must seek *fellowship forgiveness* (1 John 1:5–10). If our sins have brought public disgrace to the church, we also need *family forgiveness* (1 Cor. 5). If anyone has sinned against us and sincerely asks for forgiveness, we must forgive them. "And be kind to one another, tenderhearted, forgiving one another, even as God in Christ forgave you" (Eph. 4:32).

Those of us who have been forgiven must also be forgiving. An unforgiving spirit can hinder my praying (Matt. 5:21–26; 1 Pet. 3:7) and give the enemy a foothold in my life (Eph. 4:25–27). "If I regard iniquity in my heart, the Lord will not hear [me]" (Ps. 66:18). When we forgive others, it takes the burden from our minds and hearts and enables the Holy Spirit to work in us and through us.

Forgiveness breaks down walls, builds bridges, and heals wounds. King David knew this, and that's why he prayed as he did. "Make me to hear joy and gladness, that the bones You have broken may rejoice. . . . Restore to me the joy of Your salvation" (Ps. 51:8, 12).

Forgiveness brings freedom, and freedom brings joy.

The Joy of Suffering for Jesus

I once heard a preacher say to his congregation, "If you want to get rid of all your problems and burdens, give yourself to Jesus!" I wanted to stand up and say, "And you will be given a whole new set of burdens and problems!" After all, Jesus did say, "In the world you will have tribulation" (John 16:33), and Peter wrote to Christians in his day to "[cast] all your care upon Him, for He cares for you" (1 Pet. 5:7). He told them that a "fiery trial" was coming and that they would suffer for being Christians (4:12–16).

I have a feeling that the church today will be facing a fiery trial that will separate the sheep from the goats and the real disciples from the counterfeits. The early church suffered greatly at the hands of godless people and yet they rejoiced that they were "counted worthy to suffer shame for His name" (Acts 5:41). Peter told the suffering saints to rejoice in times of persecution because that's the way the world treated Jesus. When the world starts to treat us as it treated Him, we have been promoted! Peter told them to trust the Holy Spirit to help them and show them ways to glorify God (1 Pet. 4:12–16). Genuine Christians are like light and salt, and the unsaved don't like to have their evil words and deeds exposed and condemned by the walk and witness of the people of God.

But I wonder if the church today is prepared for the fiery furnace? If we are not prepared, we will not be able to witness to the lost or maintain our Christian joy in the midst of pain, false accusation, and possible imprisonment and death. As you read 2 Corinthians 6:1–10, ask God to examine your heart and show you how to prepare.

The Joy of Living in and by the Scriptures

Most of my life, I have been privileged to devote myself to the Bible, the Word of God; for this blessing, I praise the Lord. A few days after I was saved, I visited the public library for Bible study helps and found a study Bible on the shelf. I had never seen one before! I don't know how long the book had been there, but I was the first person to take it out.

I have read through the Bible many times in various versions, I have studied it personally and in the seminary classroom, and I have taught it to church congregations, ministerial conferences, and seminary classes. I have meditated on Scripture daily in my early morning devotional time and have sought to obey it the rest of each day. I read other books, of course, but I test them by what the Bible says. Over the years, I have written many commentaries on the Scriptures and on biblical themes.

I say all this only to assure you that I love God's Word and rejoice at the privilege of sharing it with others. The world offers nothing to match the joys God's people receive from their personal adventures with their Bibles. It's the joy of a starving, fainting traveler who sits down to eat a nutritious meal. Moses told the Israelites that "man shall not live by bread alone; but man lives by every word that proceeds from the mouth of the LORD" (Deut. 8:3). When Satan tempted Jesus to turn stones into bread, our Lord defeated him by quoting this verse (Matt. 4:1–4).

The Word of God is spiritual food that gives life, strength, and spiritual health to God's children who feed upon it. God's Word is compared not only to bread but also to milk (1 Pet. 2:1–3), solid food (Heb. 5:12–14), and honey (Ps. 19:10; 119:103). If you can't make a meal out of bread, milk, meat, and honey, you have probably been starving with the prodigal in the far country (Luke 15:11–24). We all need to follow the example of Job, who said, "I have treasured the words of His mouth more than my necessary food" (Job 23:12), and of the prophet Jeremiah, who wrote, "Your words were found, and I ate them, and Your word was to me the joy and rejoicing of my heart" (15:16).

The Word of God is not a luxury; it is a necessity. It is light in the darkness to guide the pilgrim (Ps. 119:105, 130), and medicine for the sick and afflicted (107:20). The Word of God is seed (Luke 8:11) that produces fruit when it is planted in good soil and patiently cultivated. It is water that makes us clean within (Eph. 5:25–28) and a treasure that enriches our lives for time and eternity (Ps. 119:14, 72, 127, 162). The Bible is also a sharp living sword that always defeats the wicked one when wielded by faith (Eph. 6:17; Heb. 4:12). There are other metaphors for the Bible, but these examples bear witness to the necessity *and the enjoyment* of living in the Word of God. Until we come to the place where we enjoy the Scriptures and delight in them, we will never really know God's power in our lives (Ps. 119:16, 111, 162, 165). "The statutes of the LORD are right, rejoicing the heart" (19:8).

The Joy of Giving

Paul was gathering a love offering from the Gentile churches to assist the needy Jewish believers in the Holy Land, and the church in Corinth had been slow in responding. Paul devoted chapters 8 and 9 of 2 Corinthians to encouraging the Corinthian believers to keep their promises, and he used the generosity of the Macedonian churches to challenge them. He told the Corinthians "that in a great trial of affliction the abundance of [the Macedonians'] joy and their deep poverty abounded in the riches of their liberality" (2 Cor. 8:2). That is quite a formula! A great trial of affliction + deep poverty + God's grace = abounding liberality and joy. The Macedonian churches were responding to the grace of God in their lives (v. 1), for the grace of giving produces in us the joy of living, and we want to give more!

Jesus said, "It is more blessed to give than to receive" (Acts 20:35), and He Himself set the example we must follow. "For you know the grace of our Lord Jesus Christ, that though He was rich, yet for your sakes He became poor, that you through His poverty might be rich" (2 Cor. 8:9). God's people are to be channels, not reservoirs. Sir Winston Churchill said, "We make a living by what we get, but we make a life by what we give." Covetousness and selfishness clog the channels of blessing God wants to open for us, and we are the losers.

Jesus first gave Himself as a servant and "went about doing good" (Acts 10:38), and then He gave Himself as a sacrifice for our sins by dying on the cross (Gal. 1:4). The Macedonians "first gave themselves to the Lord, and then to us by the will of God" (2 Cor. 8:5). *Until we give ourselves wholly to the Lord, the "joy formula" will not work for us!* Ananias and his wife Sapphira secretly calculated and hypocritically counterfeited a gift for the Lord, and the Lord took their lives (Acts 5:1–11). God "gives us richly all things to enjoy" (1 Tim. 6:17), and enjoyment must always lead to employment as we share with others what God gives to us.

"Give, and it will be given to you: good measure, pressed down, shaken together, and running over will be put into your bosom. For with the same measure that you use, it will be measured back to you" (Luke 6:38). If you like these terms—start investing!

The Joy of Anticipating Heaven

I think it was British playwright Richard Brinsley Sheridan who said, "Happiness consists in having someone to love, something to do, and something to look forward to." Every true believer has Jesus and His people to love, the work of the Lord to do, and a home in heaven to anticipate. Unfortunately, we don't usually talk about heaven unless somebody is terminally ill or has died. The fact that we don't discuss heaven as frequently as we should may indicate that we've gotten comfortable in this world and don't have too many service scars. Whenever God's people have confronted the enemy and contended for the faith and their lives, the prospect of eternity in heaven has encouraged and empowered them.

Christians are supposed to "rejoice in hope of the glory of God" (Rom. 5:2). Whether we go to heaven by way of the "Upper-taker" when Jesus comes or by way of the undertaker when we die (and we prefer the former), come what may, we have Christ's promise of a home in heaven (John 14:1–6). We have been "sealed with the Holy Spirit of promise, who is the guarantee of our inheritance" (Eph. 1:13–14). Paul's inspired words to the believers in Thessalonica make this very clear (1 Thess. 4:13–18).

But heaven is much more than a destination; it is also a motivation. Knowing that we will be in heaven with Jesus ought to make a difference in the way we live right now. For one thing, the assurance of heaven replaces the fear of death with the joy of the Lord. When loved ones die, God's people grieve, but not "as others who have no hope" (v. 13). There is coming a day of resurrection, reunion, and rejoicing in the heavenly city—and it will last forever!

The assurance of our heavenly home and our future likeness to Jesus should motivate us to live godly lives as we wait for His return. "And everyone who has this hope in Him purifies himself, just as He is pure" (1 John 3:3). It should also motivate us to witness and seek to lead others to Christ. "For what is our hope, or joy, or crown of rejoicing? Is it not even you in the presence of our Lord Jesus Christ at His coming? For you are our glory and joy" (1 Thess. 2:19–20). Anticipating our heavenly home ought to make us faithful in our work and our witness, knowing that Jesus will reward us one day. When we face opposition and persecution, we know that the ultimate victory will be ours. "Blessed are you when they revile and persecute you and say all kinds of evil against you falsely for My sake. Rejoice and be exceedingly glad, for great is your reward in heaven, for so they persecuted the prophets who were before you" (Matt. 5:11–12). The Old Testament patriarchs did not have easy lives, and it was their faith in God's promised heavenly city that helped to keep them going (Heb. 11:13–16). The future is your friend when Jesus is your Lord.

I could go on, but let me close with this almost forgotten joy: the joy of sharing your joy with others. Elizabeth shared her joy with her neighbors and relatives (Luke 1:57–58) and Mary's joy has blessed God's people around the world for centuries (vv. 46–55). Joys shared are joys multiplied, while sorrows shared are sorrows halved. We should be so excited about our joys in Christ and so determined to share them that we would never be caught complaining and criticizing like the people of the world. Read Luke 15 again and see how the shepherd, the woman, and the father all shared their joy with their friends and neighbors. Even though Paul was a prisoner in Rome, in danger of being executed, he rejoiced in the Lord and invited his friends in Philippi to rejoice with him (Phil. 2:17–18).

An Important Question

When Paul wrote to the troubled churches in Galatia, he asked them this question: "What has happened to all your joy?" (Gal. 4:15 TNIV). Whenever we lose our joy in the Lord, we make it easier for the enemy to attack us. We become critical and difficult to live with, and this makes it harder for us to do God's work as we should and to encourage others. The absence of a joyful heart is a symptom of deeper problems that must be solved. When we start the day discouraged and downhearted, we are asking for trouble. We should be saying, "This is the day the LORD has made; we will rejoice and be glad in it" (Ps. 118:24). God's compassions are new every morning (Lam. 3:22–23), and no matter what happened yesterday, we can make a new beginning today.

6

A Wise Life

So teach us to number our days, that we may gain a heart of wisdom.

Psalm 90:12

I saw a book advertised that promised to answer the question, "Why do smart people so often do dumb things?" I haven't read the book, but one simple answer is that there is a great difference between *knowledge* and *wisdom*. One of my professors, a brilliant man, walked into class one day totally unaware that he was wearing two hats. We thought he was doing it to illustrate some profound economic principle, but we were wrong. He simply took off both hats, put them on his desk, and began to lecture. When the class ended, he put both hats back on and walked out. I forgot the lecture but I cannot forget the hats.

Wisdom is not another name for knowledge. A great deal of knowledge is available today at the touch of a finger, thanks to the electronic devices available, but you may not find much wisdom that way. Wisdom comes from truth, and you pay a price to find it.

THIS IS THE LIFE!

"Buy the truth and do not sell it" (Prov. 23:23). Factual knowledge is very important, but it takes wisdom to identify it, categorize it, evaluate it, and apply it. *Wisdom costs something!* When I have a physical, my doctor gathers all kinds of data because he and his staff know how to run the equipment in the examining room, but it takes wisdom for him to put the facts together and evaluate them before he can tell me what they all mean. Where does his wisdom come from? It comes from training and a lifetime of experience. He's spent his life thinking, reading, listening, growing, making mistakes, and achieving successes. *Wisdom is the correct use of knowledge for the right purposes.* Wisdom is living skillfully by the principles our God has given to us. If anybody should be living a life of wisdom, it is the Christian who is following Jesus.

We Worship a Wise God

"With Him are wisdom and strength, He has counsel and understanding" (Job 12:13). People with wisdom but no strength are unable to put their wisdom to work, but people with strength and no wisdom will make a mess of everything. Our God can do what He wills and He never makes a mistake. After God revealed to Daniel the meaning of the king's dream, Daniel praised Him, saying, "Blessed be the name of God forever and ever, for wisdom and might are His" (Dan. 2:20). Through Jesus Christ, God's wisdom and power are available to us so that we can know what He wants us to do and know that He will help us do it. "Oh, the depth of the riches both of the wisdom and knowledge of God! How unsearchable are His judgments and His ways past finding out!" (Rom. 11:33).

Wisdom is the practical use of knowledge for accomplishing the will of God. The will of God is not only an expression of His love (Ps. 33:11), but it is also an expression of His wisdom. The Israelites were suffering in Egypt, but God didn't send Moses there immediately. He kept this brilliant man in Midian, *taking care of ignorant, stubborn sheep.* God was preparing Moses to lead a nation of sheep! In His divine knowledge, God knew what Moses was like and what the Israelites were like, and in His divine wisdom He prepared the one for the other. Wisdom has to do with values and priorities, and this keeps us from wasting our time fussing with trivial matters. We can look back now and better understand why certain people and events came into our lives, and we can thank the Lord for His wisdom. If I had insisted on getting my way, everything would have gone wrong and I would have missed so much.

We Live in a Universe Created and Commanded by a God of Power and Wisdom

Science is the organization and application of the wise principles and laws that God built into His creation. "The LORD by wisdom founded the earth; by understanding He established the heavens" (Prov. 3:19). "He has made the earth by His power, He has established the world by His wisdom, and has stretched out the heavens at His discretion" (Jer. 10:12). Were it not for this, the astronauts could never have made it safely to the moon and back. Man built the machine, but the Lord supplied the unchanging laws that made it work.

If we look up at night, we behold the stars that directed ships' pilots before the invention of compasses, radios, radar, sonar, and GPS. We look around and see the vitality and variety of plant life, animal life, and human life, from the tiniest seed to the gigantic sequoia and from the microscopic amoeba to the elephant or the skeleton of a dinosaur. If we examine an x-ray or watch a hospital TV screen, we see our inner machinery functioning and we are amazed. As I lay on the examining table, the hospital technician asked me if I wanted to see the inside of my stomach. "I'd rather see the inside of my room," I replied, but when I looked, I was speechless. "I will praise You, for I am fearfully and wonderfully made" (Ps. 139:14). As for the human species, we are kept alive by the minerals, plants, animals, and other resources that God has put into His creation for our good and His glory. Everything in creation shouts, "We praise a God of wisdom and power!"

I'm saying all of this to lead up to one thing: If our God is so wise and powerful that He can control the entire universe, is He not able to guide our little lives, care for us, and use us to fulfill the purposes for which He created us and saved us?

I think He can.

Then why do we waste time and energy by fretting and worrying? Can we not each day obey Romans 12:1–2 and Ephesians 6:10–18 and trust our Creator, Savior, and Father to equip us for each day and meet our every need?

I know He can.

We Find God's Wisdom Clearly Expressed in God's Word

The wisdom of God that we see operating in creation and in history can also work in our personal lives so that we delight in God's Word and God's will and seek to fulfill the purposes He has ordained for us (Eph. 2:10). "See that you walk circumspectly, not as fools but as wise, redeeming the time, because the days are evil" (5:15–16). We must make the best use of our time because we can never recall wasted hours and days. The Word of Christ must dwell in us richly (Col. 3:16) so that the indwelling Holy Spirit can use it to minister to us. The Spirit of God does not work in a vacuum, and if we want the Spirit's fullness, we must feed on the Word of God. Physical maturity is a given, but spiritual maturity is an opportunity that we can only grasp day by day as we walk with the Lord.

Psalm 119 focuses on the importance of the Scriptures in the believer's life, and these verses are especially significant. Read them carefully.

Oh, how I love Your law!
It is my meditation all the day.
You, through Your commandments, make me wiser than
    my enemies;
For they are ever with me.
I have more understanding than all my teachers,
For Your testimonies are my meditation.
I understand more than the ancients,
Because I keep Your precepts.
I have restrained my feet from every evil way,
That I may keep Your word.
I have not departed from Your judgments,
For You Yourself have taught me.
How sweet are your words to my taste,
Sweeter than honey to my mouth!
Through Your precepts I get understanding;
Therefore I hate every false way. (vv. 97–104)

This passage tells us several ways in which we can grow in wisdom and live successfully to the glory of God. One is by experience, both good and bad. Even our enemies can teach us if we pay attention to the Holy Spirit. We must be "God taught" and not "man taught," even though God may use people to instruct us. The psalmist didn't say that he *knew* more than his teachers, his enemies, and his elders, but that he *understood* more. The enemy had the facts and knew what was going on, but the psalmist had the truths behind the facts and knew *why* it was going on. "He made known His ways to Moses, His acts to the children of Israel" (103:7). I recall listening to some brilliant university professors who had mastered the facts involved in their courses, but they had completely missed the truths and principles behind those facts. If we don't see the hand of God in history, hear the voice of God in literature and the arts, and marvel at the wisdom of God in science, we have missed the most important lessons.

A knowledge of the Word of God is not only basic to a successful Christian life, but it is also basic to a good education. Almost all of the arts in Western civilization are based on the Bible. Herman Melville's classic novel *Moby Dick* opens with, "Call me Ishmael." If we don't know Genesis 16 and 21, we will miss what that important brief sentence contributes to the story. I once re-read *Moby Dick* and marked every quotation from and allusion to the Bible and found over one hundred! Christians who know the spiritual truths in the Bible can listen to the evening news and read the morning paper with more insight and discernment than the most popular newscaster. One of our best-known television anchormen used to end each program with, "And that's the way it is on_____" and he would give the date. Vance Havner would often say to the television set, "No, that's the way it *seems!*" He saw world events through different eyes. Campbell Morgan used to say that history was His story, and he was right.

In Jewish society, old age was equated with wisdom, and the psalmist claimed that he knew more than the ancients (119:100)! Generally speaking, wisdom and old age do go together, but there are exceptions. Some people grow old but never really grow up; they made a living but never learn how to make a life. They have gone through events in "the school of hard knocks" but fail to make the most of them. Alas, there are old fools as well as young fools! If you know the Bible, one of the benefits of old age is being able to look back and see the wonderful ways God kept His promises and accomplished His purposes. Someone has said that it matters not what happens to us; it's what we do with what happens to us that really matters. We may not be able to help it when people plow up our backs (129:3). What we *can* help is the kind of seeds we plant in the furrows, because that determines what kind of harvest we will reap. As we grow older, our eyesight may get dimmer *but our insight must become clearer.* "But the path of the just is like the shining sun, that shines even brighter unto the perfect day" (Prov.

4:18). To the obedient Christian, the things that count are not getting darker; they are getting brighter!

We Must Walk in the Fear of the Lord

The phrase "fear of the Lord" is found twenty-seven times in the Bible, fourteen of them in the Book of Proverbs alone. It is a key concept in biblical theology. I especially like the definition that Charles Bridges gives in his masterful exposition of Proverbs: "It is that affectionate reverence by which the child of God bends himself humbly to his Father's law."[1] It is not a paralyzing fear that stuns us but an energizing fear that stimulates us and motivates us to seek to please the Lord in everything. If you want to understand the fear of the Lord, start by reading and obeying Proverbs 2:1–5. I suggest you pause right now and do it.

The fear of God must always be joined with the grace, love, and mercy of God. If we are honest with ourselves, we know what sinners we really are. That God should love us and in His mercy and grace save us is astounding. The longer we walk in the light, the easier it is for us to see the sinful blemishes in our lives and the more we realize how undeserving we are to be called the children of God. But there is another consequence. The more we see ourselves, the more we love the Lord and want to do everything to please Him. The fear of the Lord is not only a healthy fear of divine discipline but also a fear of missing the wonderful blessings God has prepared for us. I like the phrase "affectionate reverence" that Bridges used. Wrapped up in that word "affectionate" is our feeble understanding of the cross of Christ and the love that put Him there. He loved *me*! He gave Himself for *me*! Psalm 2:11 says it perfectly: "Serve the LORD with fear, and rejoice with trembling."

1. Charles Bridges, *An Exposition of Proverbs* (Grand Rapids: Zondervan, 1959), 3–4.

"No one can know the true grace of God," said A. W. Tozer, "who has not known the fear of God." The author of the Epistle to the Hebrews wrote, "Therefore, since we are receiving a kingdom which cannot be shaken, let us have grace, by which we may serve God acceptably with reverence and godly fear. For our God is a consuming fire" (Heb. 12:28–29).

We Must Share God's Wisdom with Others

If you want to know what God thinks of the wisdom of this world, read 1 Corinthians 1:14–2:16 and take it to heart. God calls it foolishness—not that knowledge itself is foolish (although some popular ideas and theories are absurd), but the world is foolish in the way it applies knowledge. It has always been God's plan that the older generations teach the younger generations what they need to know about the important matters of life, and I fear our older Christians have been remiss in doing this. Paul told Timothy, "And the things that you have heard from me among many witnesses, commit these to faithful men who will be able to teach others also" (2 Tim. 2:2). We call this mentoring, but the Bible calls it discipling. In Greek mythology, when Odysseus went off to war, he entrusted his son to the wise teacher Mentor, and that is where our word *mentoring* comes from.

One of the joys of my so-called retirement years has been the privilege of mentoring some fine young men who are today serving the Lord and building Christ's church. One of them started a new church in a nearby city and I had the privilege of mentoring the church board over a series of weeks. I have also met one-on-one with high school and university students and we have studied the Scriptures verse-by-verse. If we don't disciple the younger generation, we have only ourselves to blame if our churches become worldly and fall apart. Not only must we teach the living Word, but we must live the Word that we teach and be encouraging examples to the young people. It's especially important that Christian parents and grandparents exercise spiritual influence on their children and grandchildren. The children and grandchildren are not only the future *of* the church but also the future *in* the church right now.

The Lord taught Paul the truth and he passed it along to Timothy. Timothy passed it along to others, who in turn shared it with the next generation. Here we have four generations of believers! If every generation were faithful in the home and the church, teaching God's truth to children and young people and new believers, false doctrine and worldly practices would not be able to get a foothold in the house of God.

"So teach us to number our days, that we may gain a heart of wisdom" (Ps. 90:12). Life is swift and short, and the time to start walking in wisdom and mentoring others is—NOW!

7

A Transparent Life

Now the purpose of the commandment is love from a pure heart, from a good conscience, and from sincere faith.

1 Timothy 1:5

A "transparent" Christian is one whose life is open, genuine, and authentic. This kind of life belongs to a believer who has nothing to hide and nothing to fear. Transparency is just the opposite of hypocrisy. The word *hypocrite* means "a play actor, one who wears a mask." In other words, a pretender. In the ancient world, actors wore various masks as they played different roles in the drama; and most of the Pharisees considered their religion just a matter of wearing masks and acting the part. The righteousness of the scribes and Pharisees was artificial and Jesus rejected it (Matt. 5:20). Read Matthew 23 for our Lord's assessment of hypocritical religious people.

In his letters, Paul used the word *conscience* twenty-one times, so it's an important subject that we dare not ignore. In our text,

Paul emphasizes a transparent life of integrity: a pure heart, a good conscience, and sincere faith. Hypocrites have divided hearts, not pure, loving hearts. Their conscience is defiled and their faith is a matter of routine acts and not the devotion of the heart.

But before I judge these people, I must examine my own inner life, especially the condition of my conscience. Conscience is that "inner window" through which God's light of truth shines to help us know right from wrong. If I do right, conscience applauds me; if I do wrong, it accuses me. If I keep violating my conscience, the window becomes dirty and the light becomes dimmer, and my relationship to my conscience deteriorates. Let's consider five admonitions that will help us to enjoy a transparent life because of a good conscience.

Emphasize Integrity—the Good Conscience

Integrity is the opposite of hypocrisy and duplicity, just as an integer (whole number) is the opposite of a fraction. The Pharisees in their thinking were double-minded and in their hearts tried to serve two masters (Matt. 6:24). Their inner person was divided. They told others what to do but didn't obey God's will themselves. They advertised their "piety" by praying aloud on the street corners and blowing trumpets when they brought offerings to the temple. Jesus knew what they were doing and tried to deliver them, but they rejected Him. Nicodemus and Joseph of Arimathea were among the few in the Jewish council who received the truth and trusted in Jesus (John 19:38–42).

A good conscience must be exercised by obedience (Acts 24:16) or it will gradually cease to function as it should. Caustic American writer H. L. Mencken defined conscience as "the inner voice that warns us that someone may be looking." But Christians don't obey because they might be seen by someone and become embarrassed, but because they know the Father always sees them and is pleased when they do His will. Our Father in heaven has many blessings laid up for us, and if we obey Him, He will open His treasury. The humblest Christian who maintains a clear conscience can be sure of God's continued blessing.

Encourage Maturity—the Weak Conscience

As we grow in grace and knowledge (2 Pet. 3:18), our conscience should also mature and become more and more discerning. God's truth doesn't change but we must grow in our understanding and applying of that truth. We must grow in knowledge and perception. When I was a new believer, a friend gave me a copy of a tract that explained that the Lord has a personal plan for my life and I must follow Him and not other people (Phil. 1:9–11). Yes, others can teach me and encourage me, but only Jesus can be my Lord. To use the examples of other Christians to excuse or defend my activities will never lead to maturity. I must allow the Spirit to develop my conscience as I pray, read the Scriptures, worship with God's people, and obey the Lord.

I have learned that there is such a thing as "geographical Christianity." A friend of mine (whom I will call Wally) was leading an American gospel team in Finland. As he and the team were going with their host to the service, Wally began to whistle a gospel chorus. "Who is preaching tonight?" asked the host, and Wally replied, "It's my turn to preach tonight." "Oh, but you can't preach!" the host exclaimed. "You just whistled, and Christians don't do that!" My friend didn't know that whistling a gospel tune was sinful in Finland. During my years of pastoral ministry, if I had used tobacco, I would probably have been fired; but I've preached in churches where pastors used tobacco and nobody was offended. Dr. D. Martyn Lloyd-Jones told me that Dr. G. Campbell Morgan sometimes smoked eight cigars a day! Eminent Baptist preacher Charles Haddon Spurgeon also used tobacco. Most church people today avoid tobacco for health reasons rather than religious reasons.

A person with a weak conscience lacks biblical knowledge and has a difficult time dealing with the question, "What is spiritual and what is worldly?" During World War II, under the auspices of the city, our high school teachers would take entire classes to a local movie theater on school time, and the students would watch an entertaining movie and a few cartoons, and then hear a patriotic pitch promoting war bonds and liberty stamps. Some of my Christian friends refused to attend because they boycotted the movies, but I noticed that after they graduated they became moviegoers.

The early church was seriously disturbed by questions relating to diets, food offered to idols, and obedience to the law of Moses. Strict Jews had one point of view and the Gentile believers (who had never been under the Jewish law) had another. Paul dealt with the problems of Christian freedom in Romans 14:1–15:13 and 1 Corinthians 8–10, and the principles he laid down still apply today. More mature Christians who understand their freedom in Christ are not to abuse that freedom by setting bad examples and causing others to stumble; neither should the immature believers criticize and condemn those who know how to use their freedom to the glory of God. It's simply a matter of growing up in the Lord.

When our children were small, my wife and I were very careful not to leave knives, pins, scissors, or other dangerous items lying about the house. When there were only the two of us, we had no such policy. Why? Because we were both experienced enough to avoid danger and use these items properly. *The difference was maturity.* It is important that new believers be taught the Word of God and how to apply its precepts and principles to their own lives. The test of maturity is freedom that is based on Bible truth and used to the benefit of the church and the glory of God. We must not make these borderline issues tests of fellowship or orthodoxy. We must obey 2 Timothy 2:2 and patiently lead new Christians into maturity.

A weak conscience makes some people overly scrupulous, and they become so involved in the minute details of right and wrong that they get out of balance and have no freedom at all. Some believers will not step on cracks in the sidewalk, and if they do they return to their starting point and begin their journey all over. Famous British writer Samuel Johnson was afflicted this way. The word *scruple* comes from the Latin and means "an irritating, sharp little stone in one's shoe." There are people who have irritating little scruples in their eating, driving, and even working, and these habits rob them of joy and sometimes of efficiency. A healthy conscience helps us establish the right values and avoid childish habits that destroy our freedom in Christ.

Avoid Impurity—the Defiled Conscience

Remember, conscience is like a window that lets God's light into the inner person, and if that window is dirty, the light will be dim.

> The lamp of the body is the eye. If therefore your eye is good [healthy], your whole body will be full of light. But if your eye is bad [diseased], your whole body will be full of darkness. If therefore the light that is in you is darkness, how great is that darkness! (Matt. 6:22–23)

Outlook determines outcome, and if our vision is blurred, our decisions will be bad and the consequences painful.

Each time we deliberately sin and fail to repent and confess our sin, we damage the effectiveness of our conscience until it can become so defiled that no light comes in at all and (even worse) the light becomes darkness. "To the pure all things are pure, but to those who are defiled and unbelieving nothing is pure; but even their mind and conscience are defiled" (Titus 1:15). A defiled mind can easily find opportunities to sin, and a defiled conscience has no problem defending the sinner.

In the Old Testament tabernacle there was a large laver that held gallons of water, and the priests washed their hands and feet at this laver as they served. There was no floor in the tabernacle, so their feet would become soiled, and their hands would become defiled from offering the various sacrifices. This laver was made from the brass mirrors donated by the women of the tribes (Exod. 38:8), and mirrors are a picture of the Word of God (James 1:22–25; 2 Cor. 3:18). To keep your mind and conscience clean, spend time reading and meditating on the Scriptures. Wash at the laver of God's Word! The Bible is a mirror that helps us see ourselves as we really are, and it is also water that cleanses us (Eph. 5:25–27). If we confess our sins, the Lord will forgive us and the blood of Jesus Christ will cleanse us from all sin (1 John 1:5–10).

To confess sin effectively means to say about it exactly what God says about it. We know what we have done, and it only makes matters worse when we try to make things look better. Sin is sin and confession to the Lord must be heartfelt confession. "*If* I have sinned" accomplishes nothing. If we don't come with a broken heart and honest confession, we have wasted our time. Prayer, worship, offerings, and good works do not bring forgiveness, but sincere repentance and confession do. Whenever we sin, we must deal with the matter immediately and claim the Lord's promise of forgiveness. Unconfessed sins that accumulate lead to the worst kind of conscience—the evil conscience.

Cultivate Sensitivity—the Evil Conscience

People with an evil conscience are described in Isaiah 5:20. "Woe to those who call evil good, and good evil; who put darkness for light, and light for darkness; who put bitter for sweet, and sweet for bitter!" The meaning of personal morality is so confused in today's world that some professed Christians boast about their repeated sins and call it "liberty."

If we want to have transparent lives, we must be serious about dealing with sin. To treat sin lightly is to treat the light sinfully, and the consequences are devastating. "He who covers his sins will not prosper, but whoever confesses and forsakes them shall have mercy" (Prov. 28:13). We can commit sin and cover it up with more sin and end up with an evil conscience, or we can confess our sins and conquer them through the blood of Jesus Christ and the power of the Spirit. We must jealously guard ourselves against losing our sensitivity to the things of the Spirit and having a hard heart and an evil conscience.

When a professed Christian surrenders to demonic doctrines, pretends to be spiritual, and repeatedly speaks hypocritical lies, he or she develops an evil conscience (1 Tim. 4:1–2). Paul says people like this have "seared" their conscience and it is no longer sensitive to the voice of God. The word *seared* refers to flesh that has been burned and calloused and has lost its feeling. These people don't hate sin and reject it; instead, they play with sin and enjoy it. If they confess any sin, their confessions are shallow and filled with excuses. They classify sins as small, medium, and large but rarely admit the greatness of their sins. Like the Pharisees in Jesus's day, they are more concerned with reputation than with character. If you confront them with the Word of God, they explain it away, with "That's *your* interpretation" as their usual defense.

The steps toward an evil conscience are listed in 1 John 1:5–10. If we lie to others (v. 6), we commit hypocrisy. If we lie to ourselves (v. 8), we become double-minded and guilty of duplicity. If we lie to God and make Him a liar (v. 10), we are in danger of apostasy! When you read the life of King Saul (1 Sam. 9–31), you see this deterioration demonstrated. Saul was a man of ability but he lacked integrity. He began well but ended in tragedy that brought the death of his sons, including godly Jonathan. We must pray daily that the Lord will help us to end well. "Therefore let him who thinks he stands take heed lest he fall" (1 Cor. 10:12).

Seek Recovery—the Restored Conscience

Believers without a healthy conscience are like ships without a compass or airplanes without radar. They are handicapped people, stumbling from failure to failure and excuse to excuse, never knowing the path God wants them to walk. Yet they can be restored!

> For if the blood of bulls and goats and the ashes of a heifer . . . sanctifies for the purifying of the flesh, how much more shall the blood of Christ, who through the eternal Spirit offered Himself without spot to God, cleanse your conscience from dead works to serve the living God? (Heb. 9:13–14)

However, it is one thing to have sins forgiven and quite something else to remove the sad consequences of those sins. Anybody can pull the nails out of the board, but only God can pull out the holes!

If I were to ask you, "What was King David's greatest sin?" you would probably say, "Committing adultery with Bathsheba and arranging for Uriah, her husband, to be slain in battle." But what about the time David broke God's law and ordered a census of the people? Seventy thousand people died in a plague because of this one willful sin (2 Sam. 24)! By committing both of these sins, David defiled his conscience and suffered under God's discipline. But Psalms 32 and 51 bear witness to the fact that David humbled himself and confessed his sins, and God forgave him. David married Bathsheba and God gave them a son—Solomon. David bought a piece of property, built an altar on it, offered a sacrifice to the Lord, and the plague stopped (2 Sam. 24:18–25). Years later, King Solomon built the Lord's temple on that piece of property!

Only the grace of God can take a man's two greatest sins and build a temple! "But where sin abounded, grace abounded much more" (Rom. 5:20).

No matter how much a child of God rebels or how far he or she may drift from the will of the Lord, God offers forgiveness. We must not delay and tempt God but seek Him "while He may be found"

(Isa. 55:6). We may suffer from the consequences of sin, but our communion with the Lord and His people can be restored. We can always make a new beginning, and the sooner we do so the better our lives and ministries will be and the more God will be glorified. "He who covers his sins will not prosper, but whoever confesses and forsakes them will have mercy" (Prov. 28:13).

May our heart's desire be that of hymn-writer Charles Wesley as he expressed it in this song, one of few written about the conscience.

> I want a principle within of watchful godly fear,
> A sensibility of sin, a pain to feel it near.
> Help me the first approach to feel of pride or wrong desire,
> To catch the wandering of my will, and quench the
>   kindling fire.
>
> From Thee that I no more may stray, no more Thy
>   goodness grieve,
> Grant me the filial awe, I pray, the tender conscience give.
> Quick as an apple of an eye, O God, my conscience make!
> Awake my soul when sin is nigh, and keep it still awake.
>
> Almighty God of truth and love, to me Thy power impart;
> The burden from my soul remove, the hardness from my
>   heart.
> O may the least omission pain my reawakened soul,
> And drive me to that grace again, which makes the
>   wounded whole.[1]

Amen and amen!

1. Charles Wesley, "I Want a Principle Within," *Hymns and Sacred Poems*, 1749.

8

A Forgiving Life

And be kind to one another, tenderhearted, forgiving one another,
even as God in Christ also forgave you.

Ephesians 4:32

After our first parents disobeyed God (Gen. 3), they tried to cover
their sin and shame and escape divine judgment, but everything
they attempted failed. They made clothing out of leaves but still
felt guilty. They tried to hide among the trees but the Lord found
them and confronted them with their sin. They tried to put the
blame on others but the Lord knew the truth. People still use these
evasive devices today to solve the sin problem, but as in Adam's
day, they only make matters worse. It was not until God shed the
blood of innocent animals and clothed the man and his wife with
skins that they were forgiven and their fellowship with God was
restored. This, of course, is a picture of what Jesus did for us on
the cross. He told His disciples, "For this is My blood of the new
covenant, which is shed for many for the remission of sins" (Matt.

26:28). "The blood of Jesus Christ His Son cleanses us from all sin" (1 John 1:7). "But You are a God, ready to pardon, gracious and merciful, slow to anger, abundant in kindness" (Neh. 9:17). He is the God who forgives.

The Lord Forgives Sinful Men

During His earthly ministry, Jesus not only healed broken bodies but also cleansed sinful hearts. Let's consider three such occasions.

A Helpless Paralytic (Matt. 9:1–8)

The four friends could not bring the helpless man into the crowded house through the door, so they made an opening in the roof and lowered him down before the Master. However, Jesus did not begin with the man's paralyzed body but rather with his sinful heart: "Son, be of good cheer; your sins are forgiven you" (v. 2). Did the man's sins have something to do with his physical condition? We don't know. But our Lord's statement greatly offended the critical religious leaders present, for in speaking it Jesus was claiming to be God. Of course it is easier to say "Your sins are forgiven you," because nobody can watch a spiritual transaction like that take place. How can you prove it happened? But Jesus was using the situation for an "action sermon." The paralyzed man was a picture of the lost sinner, unable to heal himself and totally at the mercy of God. Jesus healed both soul and body, and the physical healing demonstrated the reality of the spiritual healing.

Jesus does have the authority both to forgive sins and to heal bodies. I have visited many sick and handicapped people who would have welcomed healing but who had no interest in receiving Jesus as Lord and Savior. Apparently Jesus saw that the paralyzed man had faith. Physical healing lasts but a short time, while salvation is a gift for eternity. When we call upon Him, Jesus forgives sins and grants eternal life, for "whoever calls on the name of the LORD shall be saved" (Acts 2:21).

Some Heedless People

As the Roman soldiers were nailing Jesus to the cross, He repeatedly prayed, "Father, forgive them, for they do not know what they do" (Luke 23:34). The soldiers, of course, were only routinely obeying orders, but the Jewish officials who engineered our Lord's death were sinning against a flood of light. They knew the prophets, they had seen the miracles, and they had heard our Lord's messages, yet they rejected Him and asked to have Him killed. Jesus prayed that the Father would grant forgiveness to the ignorant Roman soldiers and also the arrogant religious leaders. This does not mean they were automatically saved and went to heaven, but that the Father would hold back the judgment they deserved and give them opportunity to be saved. In Old Testament days a man who merely touched the ark of God was instantly slain by the Lord (2 Sam. 6:1–7), yet here were men nailing the Son of God to a cross! Ignorance is no excuse in the sight of the law. The Jewish religious leaders and the Roman authorities were ignorant and guilty, but God in His grace held back the judgment. He gave Jerusalem about forty years of grace before the Roman army came and destroyed it. During that period of grace, thousands of people became Christians in Jerusalem, Judea, and Samaria, including a great many priests (Acts 6:7). Jesus had "made intercession for the transgressors" (Isa. 53:12) and the Father heard and answered. Jesus forgave His enemies and is a good example for us to follow. When the Jews stoned Stephen to death, he prayed, "Lord, do not charge them with this sin" (Acts 7:60). God can give us the grace to forgive and forget so we can become more like Jesus.

A Helpless Criminal (Luke 23:38–43)

God in His providence arranged for the cross of Jesus to stand between the crosses on which the two criminals were hanging. Both could hear Him speak and both could read the inscription that Pilate had written and put over His head: "Jesus of Nazareth, King of the Jews." One of the thieves seemed angry and defiant, but the other one realized that Jesus was not a criminal but a king, and turned to Him for help. The man admitted his own guilt and believed that Jesus could give him entrance into His kingdom. Jesus heard his prayer and gave him his request. The criminal didn't know when Jesus would ascend the throne, but our Lord said it would be that very day! Jesus gave up His life before the other men died and therefore was able to welcome the helpless thief to paradise. The first Adam became a thief and was cast out of paradise, but the Last Adam died for a thief and took him to paradise!

People assume that this was the last opportunity the thieves had to believe in Jesus, but it's possible that this was their *first* opportunity. The one thief did not waste his opportunity but by faith turned to Jesus for salvation. It's very dangerous for unsaved people to assume they have plenty of time to trust Jesus and be saved, for we never know when life will end. Scripture does not tell us what the other thief did. We trust that he too was saved.

The Lord Forgives Sinful Women

We have interesting accounts of our Lord's ministry to three "sinful women" who trusted the Savior and experienced new beginnings.

A Contrite Woman (Luke 7:36–50)

Why Simon the Pharisee invited Jesus to dine with him and then failed to honor Him as a guest is a puzzle to us. Was it an attempt to humiliate Him? If so, just think of how humiliated Simon must have been when "the woman who was a sinner" came into the room and began to do for Jesus everything that Simon had not done! The woman was guilty of sins of the flesh, but Simon was guilty of sins of the spirit: pride, criticism of the woman and of Jesus, and lack of love. Simon neglected to show common courtesy to Jesus, while the woman poured out her love on the Savior openly and without shame. Jesus was called "a friend of tax collectors and sinners" (v. 34) and the title did not embarrass Him. If you consult a harmony of the Gospels, you will find that this event followed our Lord's public invitation recorded in Matthew 11:28–30, "Come unto me . . . and I will give you rest." The woman heard that invitation, believed in Jesus and was forgiven, and brought her devotion to Him. "Your sins are forgiven," Jesus told her. "Your faith has saved you. Go in peace" (Luke 7:48, 50). By faith, she received the gift of forgiveness that brought salvation and peace to her heart.

A Cautious Woman (John 4:1–42)

Jesus was in Samaria with His disciples and met this woman at Jacob's well while the Twelve went to buy food. It was unusual for a Jewish rabbi to converse with a woman in public, especially a woman of her reputation and a Samaritan at that. To open a conversation, Jesus asked her for a drink of water. This startled her, for "the Jews have no dealings with the Samaritans" (v. 9). But it gave Jesus opportunity to introduce her to the living water of eternal life. As you read the conversation between the woman and Jesus, note how cautious she is in her questions and her answers. In her mind she was probably saying, *This man is different and I wonder what He's really up to.* She grew in her knowledge of Jesus, from "a Jew" (v. 9) to "greater than Jacob" (v. 12) to "a prophet" (v. 19) to "the Christ" (v. 29). When Jesus asked about her husband, she cautiously denied having a husband, but Jesus knew the truth and told her so. She trusted the Savior and went immediately into the city where she told the men she had met the Messiah. Jesus remained with them for two days and many were saved. Could Jesus save a woman who had been divorced four times, remarried three times, and was at that time attached to a "live-in" mate? Of course He can—and He did! And He is still saving sinners, for He is the Savior who seeks and saves the lost.

A Condemned Woman (John 8:1–12)

Everything about this event disturbs me, except for the salvation of this anonymous woman. It's obvious that the whole thing was a plot to trap our Lord. Where was the man who was involved in this act of adultery? Obviously he was paid to lure the woman into sin and then he deserted her. It's incredible that *religious* leaders conceived this plot and brought the woman *into the temple* where they confronted Jesus. They interrupted His message as they placed the woman in the midst of the listening crowd. Why did Jesus write with His finger on the ground? What did He write? Did He write the law of Moses that had originally been written on stone tablets by the finger of God (Exod. 31:18)? Perhaps Jesus was reminding these scholars of Jeremiah 17:13, a word of warning from the Lord: "Those who depart from Me shall be written in the earth, because they have forsaken the LORD, the fountain of living waters." The religious leaders who opposed Jesus had departed from the truth and forsaken the Lord, yet here they were trying to trap Jesus and have this woman stoned. Jesus didn't preach a sermon or do a miracle. All He said was, "He who is without sin among you, let him throw a stone at her first" (John 8:7). Stabbed by their own conscience, the accusers left the temple one by one. Lovingly, Jesus said to her, "Neither do I condemn you; go and sin no more" (v. 11). "There is therefore now no condemnation to those who are in Christ Jesus" (Rom. 8:1).

The Lord Forgives Believers Who Have Sinned

God's children are not sinless, but they do sin less and less as they grow in the Lord and walk in the Spirit. As our heavenly High Priest, Jesus can give us the grace we need to overcome temptation (Heb. 4:14–16). But if we fail to trust Him and deliberately sin, He is our Advocate with the Father. If we confess our sins, He will forgive us and restore us to fellowship with the Father (1 John 1:9–2:2). We have already considered God's dealing with David's sins. Now let's consider three of God's champions who disobeyed the Lord but found forgiveness.

Abraham Flees to Egypt (Gen. 12:10–13:1)

Abraham is the great biblical example of a man of faith (Rom. 4; Heb. 11:8–19). By faith he and his wife left their home in Ur of the Chaldees and went to Canaan, the land God gave them. No sooner did they arrive than they discovered a famine in the land. Why would God lead them into that kind of a situation? One reason was to test them so they would learn to walk by faith and not by sight. God knew their hearts but they didn't know their own hearts, and a faith that can't be tested can't be trusted. Early in their faith journey with the Lord, they had to discover that times of testing can become times of blessing.

At this point we must notice that most leaders in Scripture failed in their strong points, not their weak points. Abraham the man of faith failed to trust God and fled to Egypt. Moses the meek man (Num. 12:3) lost his temper and struck the rock, and David the man of integrity got caught in a web of disobedience and deception. Peter was a courageous man who wilted before a servant girl and denied the Lord. Paul wrote, "For when I am weak, then I am strong" (2 Cor. 12:10). The safest place in the world is in the will of God, no matter what the circumstances around us may be.

When Abraham arrived in famine-stricken Canaan, he should have said, "The Lord brought us here and He will care for us."

Then he should have built his altar and worshiped the Lord, and pitched his tents as witnesses that he was a stranger and pilgrim in the land. Instead he headed for Egypt, where he lied to the king and almost lost his wife. The fulfillment of the Messianic prophecy was at stake! Abraham's taking Lot to Egypt ruined Lot's walk of faith and he began to measure everything by what he had seen in Egypt (Gen. 13:10). As a result, Lot eventually lost everything.

The people of Israel were prone to follow Abraham's bad example, just as some Christians do today. Whenever there was trouble during their wilderness journey, the Israelites wanted to go back to Egypt. Whether they were hungry or thirsty or being attacked by enemies, their first response was to look back to Egypt and not look up to the Lord. They would rather be in bondage and have security than be set free and trust the Lord. Centuries later the prophet Isaiah had to warn their descendants, "Woe to those who go down to Egypt for help" (Isa. 31:1).

Abraham lost his testimony and got into serious trouble in Egypt because of his lies and unbelief. After all, God blesses faith and truth and not our clever schemes. The Lord protected Sarah, rescued her and her husband, and took them back to the Promised Land where they belonged. How gracious He is to His people!

Moses Smites the Rock (Num. 20:1–13)

Shortly after the nation of Israel marched out of Egypt, Moses provided fresh water for them by speaking to the rock (Exod. 17:1–7). After their rebellion at Kadesh, they began to complain again and this upset Moses; the Lord told him to speak to the rock and water would come forth. But Moses was angry and called the people "rebels," and with Aaron took the credit for supplying the water. In his anger he smote the rock instead of speaking to it. The Lord graciously provided the water but at the same time chastened Moses and would not permit him to enter the land of Canaan. Like Jonah outside the city of Nineveh (Jon. 4), it's possible to be a blessing to others and yet miss the blessing yourself. Those who serve the Lord must beware of excusing a temper tantrum and calling it "righteous indignation." One evening at a conference, I listened to a preacher give vent to his anger, and though his exposition had merit, his bitter attitude created a sterile atmosphere of growing discomfort. God in His love chastened Moses but centuries later allowed him to enter the land *on the Mount of Transfiguration* (Matt. 17:1–8)! "But where sin abounded, grace abounded much more" (Rom. 5:20).

Peter Denies the Lord Three Times (Luke 22:31–34, 54–62)

If Abraham was overcome by the world (Egypt) and Moses by the flesh (temper), then Peter was attacked by the devil. Jesus warned Peter that Satan was plotting against him and his fellow disciples, but Peter's self-confidence was not shaken (Luke 22:31–34). We think we know our own hearts, but we don't (Jer. 17:9), and when we feel the strongest, we are usually the weakest. "Therefore let him who thinks he stands take heed lest he fall" (1 Cor. 10:12). When you trace Peter's steps from the upper room to his shameful denials in the courtyard, you discover some of the traps that Satan sets to catch his prey. Peter was boasting when he should have been listening, sleeping when he should have been watching and praying, attacking when he should have been submitting, and following when he should have gone away. "Let these go their way" (John 18:8) was the Lord's signal to the men to get out quickly and not follow Him. Had Peter obeyed, he could have saved himself from temptation, sin, and sorrow. But after the resurrection, the Lord met Peter privately and restored his fellowship (1 Cor. 15:5); and then He met with him publicly and restored his discipleship (John 21:15–25). "Follow Me" was our Lord's announcement that all was well again. The Lord forgave Peter, filled him with the Holy Spirit, and used him to win thousands of people to faith in Jesus

Christ. The enemy accusing us wants us to believe that our sins permanently disqualify us from serving the Lord, but 1 John 1:9 shuts his mouth.

The Lord Wants Us to Forgive Others

One of the best ways to prove our faith in Christ is to forgive others when they sin and to help restore them to fellowship with the Lord and His people. If we don't forgive, we will end up needing forgiveness ourselves! "Brethren, if a man is overtaken in any trespass, you who are spiritual restore such a one in a spirit of gentleness, considering yourself lest you also be tempted" (Gal. 6:1). Private sins must be dealt with privately, public sins publicly, and all things must be done lovingly. Peter asked Jesus how many times he should forgive people their sins against him, and Jesus told him not to count the times at all (Matt. 18:21–35). By the time we have forgiven somebody 490 times, we will be in the habit of forgiveness! I use the Lord's Prayer in my daily devotional time and when I pray the fifth petition, I add, "Father, please give me a forgiving spirit today." An unforgiving spirit is a beachhead the devil can easily turn into a battleground, whether it's a careless driver, a slow elevator, a noisy child in church, or a meddling neighbor. (We once had neighbors across the street who sat on their front porch with binoculars, scanning the neighborhood. We kept our front blinds closed.)

Unforgiving believers grieve the Lord and rob themselves of blessing. I knew a church officer who actually kept in his pocket a notebook with the names of the people who had offended him or disagreed with him. He should have settled those matters immediately and enjoyed freedom, but he seemed to have overlooked 1 Corinthians 13:5, "[love] keeps no record of wrongs" (TNIV). Paul's logic in Ephesians 4:32 is so clear that we can't argue with it: since the Lord has graciously forgiven us, we should graciously forgive others. "Bearing with one another, and forgiving one another, if anyone has a complaint against another; even as Christ forgave you, so you also must do" (Col. 3:13). An unforgiving spirit hinders our praying (Matt. 5:21–26; 6:5–15; 1 Pet. 3:7) and gives the devil opportunity to attack (2 Cor. 2:6–11). We must forgive our enemies and seek to make them friends and fellow believers (Matt. 5:43–48; Rom. 12:17–21).

Forgiveness means freedom, an unforgiving spirit means bondage, and we make the decision between the two. If we choose to carry grudges and be vindictive, we are trying to "play God" and failing to love others as we should. First we must forgive in our hearts, and then we must seek to forgive personally and make matters right. Matthew 18:15–20 tells us the steps to follow.

9

A Fruitful Life

I am the vine, you are the branches. He who abides in Me, and I in Him, bears much fruit; for without Me you can do nothing.

John 15:5

Please read John 15:1–17. Our Lord's words to His disciples are ominous: "for without Me you can do nothing" (v. 5). After all, those men were to take His place after He returned to the Father, and they wanted to succeed. In the Sermon on the Mount He had warned them that flavorless salt was "good for nothing" (Matt. 5:13), and they had heard Him say that "the Son can do nothing of Himself" (John 5:19). It was in the upper room that He explained to them how to succeed in Christian service, and the principles He laid down still apply today.[1]

1. Some of the material in this chapter has been adapted from my book 5 *Secrets of Living* (Wheaton, IL: Tyndale, 1978).

If We Want to Experience Real Life, We Must Be Fruitful

The disciples were quite familiar with the metaphor Jesus used, because vines, grapes, and wine were vitally important to the Jewish way of life. A cup of wine and a piece of bread would be a laborer's lunch, and wine was usually on the table at other meals. Christianity is not just a religious way of life; it is life—and where there is life, there should be fruit. Jesus once cursed a fig tree that had no fruit and nothing but leaves (Matt. 21:19).

The Lord has left His people here on earth that they might "be fruitful and multiply" by bringing others to faith in Christ. Paul was anxious to visit Rome so that he "might have some fruit" among the Gentiles (Rom. 1:13). Paul was an evangelist, and the burden of his heart was the winning of the lost, both Jews and Gentiles. "Woe is me if I do not preach the gospel!" (1 Cor. 9:16). Is the church today burdened to reach the lost?

Godly living is another kind of fruit we should bear. Paul admonished the Romans to "have . . . fruit to holiness" (Rom. 6:22), and he urged the believers in Corinth to continue "perfecting holiness in the fear of God" (2 Cor. 7:1). The Pharisees had an artificial holiness, a brittle piety that had nothing to do with the life of God. The Holy Spirit dwells within each believer, and as we walk in the Spirit, we are able to bear the fruit of the Spirit which is "love, joy, peace, longsuffering, kindness, goodness, faithfulness, gentleness, self-control" (Gal. 5:22–23). Hebrews 12:11 speaks of "the peaceable fruit of righteousness."

Generosity is a kind of spiritual fruit that every believer should bear. The Jewish believers in Palestine were in dire straits, and to assist them, Paul took up a special offering from the Gentile churches he had founded. He referred to the offering as "this fruit" (Rom. 15:28), for it flowed out of the spiritual life of the churches. When the ushers take up the Sunday offering, they are harvesting the fruit of the spiritual lives of the worshipers. The offering is

91

"fruit," not "loot." It does not come from shallow sentiment or human pressure but from love.

When we truly praise the Lord because the Spirit is at work in our lives, this is spiritual fruit. Hebrews 13:15 calls it "the sacrifice of praise . . . the fruit of our lips, giving thanks to His name." Worship leaders devise all sorts of techniques to encourage congregations to praise the Lord, but the fault lies in the human heart. The life of God is not at work in the hearts of the people and they cannot produce the fruit of praise. The same diagnosis applies to the lack of service given in many churches. Paul called the results of his own service for the Lord "fruit from my labor" (Phil. 1:22).

Professed Christians who are not bearing fruit are either counterfeits or are not depending on the Holy Spirit, *and they are not experiencing real life!*

If We Want to Be Fruitful, We Must Abide in Jesus Christ

You can manufacture golf balls or automobiles, but you cannot manufacture fruit, because *fruit comes from life*. Fruit has in it the seeds for more fruit. In Christian circles, we hear a great deal about "results," but "results" are not the same as fruit. An accountant can get results from a computer or a housewife from a dishwasher, but that's not the same as seeing fruit from the working of the Holy Spirit. Paul admonishes us to "work out your own salvation with fear and trembling, for it is God who works in you both to will and to do for His good pleasure" (Phil. 2:12–13). God works in and we work out. Jesus told His disciples that He works in us through the Scriptures (John 15:3, 7), our obedience (vv. 10, 14), our love for one another (vv. 12–13), and prayer (vv. 7, 16).

Abiding in Christ is both a privilege and a responsibility. Our union with Christ (sonship) was accomplished when we trusted Him as Savior and Lord, but our communion (fellowship) is a moment by moment and day by day experience. It means yielding to the Spirit of God, feeding on the Word of God, worshiping the Lord, and serving where He leads us. Sometimes our deepest fellowship occurs when circumstances are difficult and the skies are dark. The vines bear the best grapes when they have been carefully pruned, and God has to cut away from us those things that rob us of both quality and quantity in our fruit-bearing (vv. 1–2). *The Father is closest to us when He is trimming us.* The process is painful, but without it we cannot be fruitful.

How do we know when we are abiding? For one thing, we are bearing fruit and bringing glory to His name. Our hidden resources in Christ are enabling us to mature and minister in ways that amaze us. We have love and joy in our hearts and give praise and thanksgiving to the Father as we do our work. We see God answering prayer and we sense His presence with us even in the darkest hours. We find joy in making sacrifices as we serve others. In short, we become more like Jesus and seek to share Him with the lost.

Unbelief and deliberate sin break our fellowship with the Lord. When that happens, we become impatient, selfish, demanding, critical, and unfruitful—*and we know it!* That's when we must get alone with the Lord in heart and mind, confess our sins, and get back into communion with the Master. Recalling biblical promises and claiming them is great medicine for the soul. To allow ourselves to remain out of fellowship is to invite the chastening hand of God to discipline us, because the Father loves us too much to let us break our fellowship, cripple our walk, and destroy our fruit (Heb. 12:1–17). We must pray with King David, "Restore to me the joy of Your salvation" (Ps. 51:12).

If We Want to Abide in Christ, We Must Obey Him

The Lord has written into His creation certain principles and laws that must be obeyed if we want to succeed. Did these laws not exist, science would collapse and the machinery of life would stand still. Airplanes fly because they are built to obey the laws of aerodynamics; automobiles move because the motor obeys the laws of internal combustion; medicines heal because they work along with the principles of digestion, circulation, and so forth in the human body. But what is true in the world of science is also true in the spiritual world. "If you keep My commandments," said Jesus, "you will abide in My love" (John 15:10). "You are My friends if you do whatever I command you" (v. 14). To jump from a skyscraper and defy the law of gravity is suicide, and to disobey the laws of God is to rob ourselves of the power, wisdom, and joy He wants us to have.

Our attitude toward the will of God must be one of joyful, loving obedience. This is what the Son said to the Father: "I delight to do Your will, O my God, and Your law is within my heart" (Ps. 40:8; see Heb. 10:5–9). If I picture God's will as a restrictive bit and bridle (Ps. 32:9) or as uncomfortable bonds (2:3), I will never enter into the joys and victories of His will. Remember, the will of God comes from the heart of God and is an expression of His personal love for us (33:11). Pruning is not a comfortable experience, but we submit to it because we love Him and want to please Him. The useless foliage in our lives is only hindering the production of fruit that glorifies God.

Some Christians harbor wrong ideas about the will of God. They think God's will applies only to "important things," like choosing a career or finding a life's mate; but God's will applies to all aspects of life. This doesn't mean we must pray about what tie we wear or what color car we buy, for our sanctified common sense assists us here. Proverbs 3:5–6 tells us not to lean on our own understanding, but we aren't told to abandon it! God created us in His image to be reasonable creatures, and knowledge and wisdom always work together.

If We Want to Obey Him, We Must Love Him

Without love, obedience can become a heavy burden that grinds us down; but with love, we gladly do the will of God. "For this is the love of God, that we keep His commandments. And His commandments are not burdensome" (1 John 5:3). Jesus said, "If you keep My commandments, you will abide in My love" (John 15:10), and as we abide in His love, we keep His commandments! The account of Jacob's love for Rachel comes to mind (Gen. 29:20). If we obey the Lord only to escape chastening, or to get a reward, we are not experiencing the Christian life at the highest. Our service is punishment, not enrichment, and the joy of the Lord is not enabling us to labor. Love is the highest motive for sacrifice and service (John 15:13), and "love never fails" (1 Cor. 13:8).

What is Christian love? It is treating others the way Jesus treats us. Love is not a feeling that comes and goes. Love is an act of the will; it is deliberately living as Jesus lived, depending on the power of the Spirit to enable us. Love is the fulfillment of the law of God (Rom. 15:8–10) and delivers us from the sort of mechanical, legalistic lifestyle the Pharisees practiced. Love is a way of life, not a gimmick we turn on and off like a computer. The first fruit of the Spirit is love (Gal. 5:22), because it is in the deep, rich soil of love that the other fruit will grow. Read 1 Corinthians 13 and Galatians 5:22–23 and see how they parallel each other. Sometimes the Lord sends trials to help "fertilize" our garden of love, and we must let Him have His way. Joseph named one of his sons Manasseh, which means "one who forgets," and said, "God has made me forget all my toil and all my father's house." His other son he named Ephraim, which means "fruitfulness" (Gen. 41:51–53). Because of his faith and his love for the Lord, Joseph ignored the trials he experienced and had a fruitful ministry in Egypt—and the Lord worked everything out!

If We Want to Love Jesus More, We Must Get to Know Him Better

You can now see the sequence involved in the fruitful Christian life.

The better we know Jesus, the more we will love Him.

95

The more we love Him, the more we will obey Him.

The more we obey Him, the deeper we will abide in Him.

The deeper we abide in Him, the more fruit we will bear.

The more fruit we bear, the more we will experience real life in abundance.

The better we get to know some people, the more difficult it may be for us to like them, but the better we get to know Jesus, the more we will love Him, even though He is light years ahead of us in every way. *He is willing to fellowship with us!* Jesus touched the lepers, ate with unclean sinners, welcomed the outcasts, and finally died on the cross for undeserving lost sinners. We are imperfect, but He is perfect. We are selfish, but He unselfishly gives of Himself and all that He owns, which is everything. God's goal for our lives is that we be "conformed to the image of His Son" (Rom. 8:29). This does not mean that we exert every effort to imitate Christ, but that we yield to Him and allow the Spirit to transform us to become more and more like Him. We experience incarnation, not imitation: "Christ lives in me" (Gal. 2:20).

The work of the Holy Spirit in the world today is twofold: to convict lost people of their need for a Savior, and to transform saved people to be more like the Savior that the world needs. The two ministries go together, for the more the church is like Jesus, the more the lost world will see Jesus and want to know Him. We are the salt of the earth, *and salt makes people thirsty*. We are the light of the world, and *light helps people see things as they really are* (Matt. 5:13–16). The Lord reaches the lost by means of what His people are and what they do.

How do we get to know Jesus better? By spending time with Him daily in the Scriptures and in prayer, by fellowshipping with Him and His people regularly in worship and service, by observing the creation around us and praising Him, and by listening with our hearts to the cries for help and responding to them as God guides us. Sometimes we need to get away alone and devote uninterrupted time to communion with the Lord. When we get too busy and too involved, we are prone to become distracted and unproductive, and that's when our Lord tells us it's time to come apart and rest awhile (Mark 6:31). Whenever John Wesley's mother felt overwhelmed as she cared for her large family, she sat down, pulled her apron over her head, and meditated and prayed. This put things back together again. I've learned that taking occasional "blessing breaks" is a source of strength and peace from the Lord. Delayed at the crossing by a slow train? Standing in the check-out line while a customer searches for an elusive credit card? Waiting in a restaurant for a late friend? Let's not get impatient and complain! Let's quiet our hearts before the Lord and draw upon His grace. We waste time when we do unimportant things, but we invest time *in eternity* when we pause to pray and meditate.

To know Jesus better means to love Jesus more, and this results in our loving sin and the sinful world system less. It means loving God's people more and yearning for the lost to come to the Savior. We will love the Word of God more and constantly find Jesus on its pages.

To know Jesus better means gradually becoming more like Him, even though we may not always recognize it. We may occasionally be misunderstood by our family and friends, but never mind Jesus was also misunderstood, and so were the apostles.

Jesus understands us and we are growing in our knowledge of Him, and that's all that really matters.

10

An Exchanged Life

I have been crucified with Christ; it is no longer I who live, but Christ lives in me; and the life which I now live in the flesh I live by faith in the Son of God, who loved me and gave Himself for me.

Galatians 2:20

There are seven personal pronouns in this verse, but Paul is writing not only about himself but also about every person who has trusted Jesus Christ as Savior and Lord. He is explaining an incredible spiritual transaction that, if we understand it and claim it, will transform our lives. I read about a Civil War veteran who was living in poverty but was proud of the fact that he had a "letter signed by Mr. Lincoln." Another veteran looked at the letter and said, "This letter guarantees you a pension for the rest of your life! Why are you living in poverty?" Too many Christians are stumbling along in spiritual poverty and defeat when Jesus has already provided for their every need!

Our old life, before we knew Christ, was an enslaved life; but our new life in Christ is an exchanged life. According to Galatians 2:20, this is what that means:

- We have exchanged being dead *in* sin (Eph. 2:1) for being dead *to* sin, because we have been crucified with Christ.

- We have exchanged being energized by Satan for being empowered by Christ, because we live in Christ and He lives in us.

- We have exchanged walking by sight (as the world does) for walking by faith, for we live by faith in the Son of God.

- We have exchanged being motivated by selfishness for being motivated by God's love, because Jesus loved us and gave Himself for us.

We Have Exchanged Being Dead in Sin for Being Dead to Sin through Jesus Christ

There are two aspects of Christ's work on the cross that must be distinguished. First, it was a work of *substitution*. Our text tells us that He "loved me and gave Himself for me." Jesus "bore our sins in His own body on the tree" (1 Pet. 2:24). Jesus said, "I lay down My life for the sheep" (John 10:15). This is the good news of the gospel, that "Christ died for our sins according to the Scriptures, and that He was buried, and that He rose again the third day according to the Scriptures" (1 Cor. 15:3–4). Under the old covenant, the sheep died for the shepherds; but under the new covenant, the Good Shepherd died for the sheep! This is substitution.

Our text closes with substitution but it opens with *identification*: "I am crucified with Christ." Paul explains substitution in Romans 5, while in Romans 6 he explains identification. When we trusted Christ, the Holy Spirit baptized us, or identified us with, the body of Christ (1 Cor. 12:13) so that we have died with Christ, our old life has been buried with Christ, we arose with Christ, we ascended with Christ, and today we are seated with Christ and are sharing in the riches of His grace (Eph. 2:4–6). Through the indwelling Holy Spirit, every believer is identified with Jesus, so that 1 John 4:17 affirms that "as He is, so are we in this world." We are so identified with Christ that, when Saul of Tarsus persecuted the believers, he was actually persecuting Jesus Christ (Acts 9:4)!

If we are identified with Christ, what bearing does this have on our day-by-day, practical Christian life? Consider these biblical truths.

"And those who are Christ's have crucified the flesh with its passions and desires" (Gal. 5:24).

"Therefore we were buried with Him through baptism into death, that just as Christ was raised from the dead by the glory of the Father, even so we also should walk in newness of life" (Rom. 6:4).

"But God forbid that I should glory except in the cross of our Lord Jesus Christ, by whom the world has been crucified to me, and I to the world" (Gal. 6:14).

"Having disarmed principalities and powers, He made a public spectacle of them, triumphing over them in it [the cross]" (Col. 2:15).

These verses make it clear that our spiritual enemies—the world, the flesh, and the devil (Eph. 2:1–2)—have been defeated by our Lord's death, resurrection, ascension to heaven, and enthronement in heaven! As by faith we identify with Christ's victories, the Holy Spirit enables us to triumph. "For whatever is born of God overcomes the world. And this is the victory that has overcome the world—our faith" (1 John 5:4; see v. 18). We have died to the old covenant law (Gal. 2:19) so that we live by God's grace in all that we are and all that we do (1 Cor. 15:10; 2 Cor. 12:9).

A physically dead person cannot respond to physical stimuli, and a person who has been crucified with Christ need not respond to stimuli from the world, the flesh, and the devil. We are to reckon ourselves dead to sin (Rom. 6:1–14), which means that we should believe that what God says in the Bible about all believers is true for ourselves. It's like cashing a check. Suppose I give a missionary friend a check to help support his ministry. He believes there is money in my account to cover it, so he goes to the bank, endorses the check, and receives the money. As children of God, we believe God's Word that we are identified with Christ in His victories, so we claim victory by faith. We endorse the check! When we are tempted by the world, the flesh, or the devil, we deal with it like victors and not victims, and trust the Lord for overcoming power.

We died with Christ and therefore can reject the temptations hurled at us by our enemies. We arose with Christ and therefore have spiritual life and power now. We ascended with Christ and therefore are not of this world even though we are in this world. We are enthroned with King Jesus in heaven and therefore have authority to "reign in life" (Rom. 5:17). If we put a snakelike letter *s* just after the *e* in reign, we end up with "resign." To yield to temptation is to abandon our throne, and it isn't worth it!

Salvation means coming to the cross to trust Christ, but discipleship means carrying the cross and identifying with Jesus Christ. "If anyone desires to come after Me," said Jesus, "let him deny himself, and take up his cross daily, and follow Me" (Luke 9:23). To carry a cross means to accept suffering and shame and to be willing to put to death those things that are not in the will of God. Today the cross is a piece of jewelry, but in the first century the Romans saw crucifixion as the lowest form of execution. Jesus transformed the cross into power and victory, and Paul gloried in the cross (Gal. 6:14)!

We Have Exchanged Being Energized by Satan for Being Empowered by Christ

The person who does not have Jesus living within has Satan, the prince of the power of the air, living within and in control (Eph. 2:2). Many people have the idea that Satan controls lost people only by means of narcotics, alcohol, pornography, covetousness, anger, and other such sins, but this is not true. Satan is basically a counterfeiter; he copies what God has to offer and most people can't tell the difference. In the parable of the tares (Matt. 13:24–30, 36–43), Satan sows counterfeit Christians wherever Jesus sows true believers. The devil has counterfeit ministers (2 Cor. 11:13–15) that declare a counterfeit gospel (Gal. 1:6–9) and encourage a false righteousness (Rom. 9:30–10:4). Eventually, he will produce a counterfeit Christ (2 Thess. 2). It's difficult to realize that some of the nicest religious people we know may not be Christians at all but servants of Satan, and, unless they turn to Christ, they will be with Satan forever.

According to Ephesians 2:1–3, unsaved people are spiritually dead, disobedient to God, and living for the world, the flesh, and the devil. This doesn't mean they do bizarre things that startle people, because Satan is much wiser than that. Judas was an apostle, in fact, the treasurer of the group, and he preached sermons and even did miracles (Luke 10:17–20), yet he was not a believer (John 6:66–71).

Christ lives in us in the person of the Holy Spirit, whom Jesus called "the Helper" (14:16, 26; 15:26; 16:7). The Helper does for believers today what Jesus did for His disciples while He was with them on earth. Satan is strong and subtle, but "He who is in you is greater than he who is in the world" (1 John 4:4), and He is always with you. The Spirit reminds us of what He has taught us from the Word and enables us to have wisdom in detecting and defeating the enemy. Satan and his demonic army cannot read your mind, so be careful what you say or write lest the enemy make use of it. However, as we obey the Lord, He will be our "refuge and strength" and see us through to victory (Ps. 46:1).

Just as God dwelt in the tabernacle and the temple, so the Spirit lives within every child of God, and we must be careful how we treat God's temple (1 Cor. 6:18–20). To abuse it, not care for it properly, or deliberately put it into unnecessary danger is to sin against the Holy Spirit. The believer's body is also God's tool chest, for the members of our body are "instruments" (or tools) for the Lord to use (Rom. 6:13–14). God used David's arm and sling to defeat a giant and the tongues of the prophets to declare His Word. The believer's body is a depository for God's spiritual wealth, for "we have this treasure in earthen vessels" (2 Cor. 4:7). The Holy Spirit has given each of us gifts and we must use them to glorify the Lord. What a tragedy when gifted believers use their gifts to entertain the world instead of to edify the church.

We Have Exchanged "Walking by Sight" for "Walking by Faith"

Four times in the Bible you will find the statement, "The just shall live by faith" (Hab. 2:4; Rom. 1:17; Gal. 3:11; Heb. 10:38). "The just" are those who have been saved by faith in Jesus Christ and have been declared righteous (justified) by the Lord. Paul's epistle to the Romans explains this miracle. Galatians explains how the just should live, and Hebrews explains what it means to walk by faith. "For we walk by faith, not by sight" (2 Cor. 5:7). To walk by faith means that God's people measure life and make decisions on the basis of God's Word and God's glory, not on the basis of what they see, hear, feel, or learn from the world in which they live. When Abraham fled to Egypt (Gen. 12:10), he was walking by sight and not by faith, and so was his nephew Lot when he and his family moved into Sodom (Gen. 13). Both families got into trouble.

The Christian life begins with an act of faith when we trust Jesus to save us. But for the Christian life to grow and be a blessing, we must maintain an attitude of faith, knowing that the Lord has a perfect plan for our lives. "And do not be conformed to this world, but be transformed by the renewing of your mind, that you may prove what is that good and acceptable and perfect will of God" (Rom. 12:2). The Lord uses the Scriptures, prayer, wise counsel, and worship to renew our minds so we will know His will and do it. When I was serving in Youth for Christ, Dr. Bob Cook used to tell us, "If you can explain what's happening in your ministry, God didn't do it. Keep your ministry on a miracle basis." There is good scriptural backing for what he said, found

THIS IS THE LIFE!

in Isaiah 55:8: "For My thoughts are not your thoughts, nor are your ways My ways."

Faith is not recklessly jumping ahead and doing what we feel is God's will. Faith is obeying God regardless of how we feel, what the circumstances are, or what the consequences may be. The founder of the China Inland Mission, J. Hudson Taylor, said, "Having faith in God is depending on the faithfulness of God." Faith must be grounded in the character of God and in the word of God, and we must obey because we want to glorify God.

Faith must operate in every area of life, not just the "religious" matters. When you read Hebrews 11, you learn that Abel worshiped by faith (v. 4), Enoch walked by faith and witnessed by faith (vv. 5–6), Noah worked by faith (v. 7), and various other people warred by faith, sacrificed by faith, and suffered by faith (vv. 35–40). As you read the annals of faith, you learn that the Lord doesn't always deliver, protect, and provide; sometimes He seems to abandon us, and we get discouraged and are tempted to start walking by sight. The exchanged life means that we hold to God's Word and wait on God's timing regardless of what the people in the world would do. To walk by sight means to look around desperately for an escape hatch or for somebody who has the resources to rescue us. To put it bluntly, *faith is living without scheming*. When you study the life of Jacob, you sometimes find him praying and pleading with God and then going off and executing his own plan. That is not walking by faith, but the Lord was gracious to him and helped him, just as he helps us today.

We Have Exchanged Being Motivated by Selfishness for Being Motivated by Love

The value of a deed can often be measured by the motive behind it, and those who enjoy the exchanged life are motivated by the love of Christ. This is not natural human love but supernatural divine

104

love, for "the love of God has been poured out in our hearts by the Holy Spirit who was given to us" (Rom. 5:5). God loves the world (John 3:16), He loves the church (Eph. 5:25–27), and He loves every believer. In fact, Jesus said that the Father loves every believer just as He loves His own Son (John 17:23, 26). Amazing! It's a personal, individual love that never changes, and nothing can separate us from that love (Rom. 8:35–39).

How did Jesus demonstrate His love when He was ministering here on earth? For one thing, He had time for individuals and didn't settle just for big public meetings. He had time for blessing the children, for meeting individual seekers like Nicodemus (John 3), for dining in homes, for helping Gentile outsiders, and for healing and encouraging the helpless. He was a servant and not a celebrity, and was willing to touch a leper and also a dead corpse. He was patient with people, including His own disciples, especially when they were debating over which of them was the greatest. One day He said of His disciples, "O faithless and perverse generation, how long must I be with you and bear with you?" (Luke 9:41).

Jesus was available to the people day and night, even when He tried to take a day off and rest. He prayed for people and taught them the Word of God. He forgave people, even while they were crucifying Him, and He fed the hungry and healed the sick and afflicted. But the greatest demonstration of His love is His death on the cross. "But God demonstrates His own love toward us, in that while we were still sinners, Christ died for us" (Rom. 5:8). When I hear people complain that God doesn't love them anymore, I ask, "Have you been to Calvary lately?"

"Now Jesus loved Martha and her sister and Lazarus" (John 11:5). Then why did He delay going to Bethany when Lazarus became ill and died? Because He had grander things in mind than simply healing His beloved sick friend. "This sickness is . . . for the glory of God, that the Son of God may be glorified through it" (John 11:4). When life is motivated by love, God gives us a heart to care, patience to wait, and the opportunity to serve others and glorify God.

When we love Jesus, we are not ashamed to show it. The apostle John is called "the disciple whom Jesus loved," but he was also the disciple who loved Jesus and let it be known. When you read chapters 13 to 21 of John's Gospel, you see John expressing that love openly. He leaned on Jesus's breast in the upper room, a demonstration of what it means to abide in His love. John stood by the cross and shared the fellowship of His sufferings and those of Mary (19:26–27), and three days later, when he heard Jesus was alive, he ran to the tomb to greet Him (20:1–10). Are we in a hurry to spend time with Jesus? It was John who first recognized Jesus standing on the shore (21:7), for love has 20/20 vision; and when Jesus told Peter to follow Him, John got up and followed also (21:20). Love for Jesus helps us love His servants, even the ones who fail. It was John who wrote that profound record we call the Gospel of John, because love always has to testify of its beloved (21:24–25).

When we think of the apostle John, we should also think of Jude 21, "keep yourselves in the love of God." How do we do this? By keeping His commandments (John 15:9–10). By leaning on His breast, loving Him, and listening to Him. By loving others. By sharing the good news of salvation. By standing at the cross courageously and carrying our own cross faithfully.

Unfortunately, there are professed Christians in churches who are "enemies of the cross of Christ" and don't live like the citizens of heaven (Phil. 3:17–21). In a letter saturated with joy, mentioning this fact made Paul weep, and we ought to weep as well.

The Lord did not call us to be apostles, but He did give us an exchanged life that can make a difference in the church.

Any volunteers?

11

A Sufficient Life

And God is able to make all grace abound toward you, that you, always having all sufficiency in all things, have an abundance for every good work.

2 Corinthians 9:8

The two words *always* and *never* must be handled with care, especially by writers, preachers, spouses, and parents. If we use these two words carelessly, we may do damage and hurt the people we are trying to help. The parent who says to a child, "You always make a mess of your room" may be telling a lie, because there were times when Junior straightened out his room and should have been commended for it. The husband or wife who says, "You never pay attention when I talk" is inviting even less attention.

But God has every right to use *always* and *never*, because He knows everything and He keeps exceedingly accurate records. Fortunately for believers, He says of us that "their sins and their lawless deeds I will remember no more" (Heb. 8:12). Whenever in God's

Word He says *always* or *never*, we had better pay close attention; for the Lord wants us to have sufficiency for everything relating to our Christian life and service—and we do! As our text says, "always having all sufficiency in all things" applies to every believer.

Let's consider some of the blessings we have that make us all sufficient.

We Can Always Be Triumphant in Christ (2 Cor. 2:14–17)

"Now thanks be to God who always leads us in triumph in Christ" (2 Cor. 2:14). In verses 14–17 Paul gives a description of a Roman "triumph," the ancients' version of our modern ticker-tape parade. If a Roman commander-in-chief had won a complete victory over an enemy on foreign soil, slain at least five thousand enemy soldiers, gained new territory for Rome, and brought home enemy officers as prisoners, he was entitled to the honor of a Roman triumph. The commander-in-chief rode in a special chariot and was cheered along with his officers, but the enemy captives were treated like slaves. The Roman priests in the parade burned incense in honor of their gods, and when the Roman soldiers smelled that fragrance, it spoke to them of life. But when the captive officers smelled the incense, it spoke to them of death, because they were going to the coliseum to face the hungry lions. Read the passage again with these facts in mind.

Our Lord and Savior Jesus Christ left heaven for foreign soil (planet Earth) and while here won a total victory over Satan, sin, and death. Every Christian is marching with Him and sharing in His victory. As I mentioned earlier, we not only fight *for* victory, but we fight *from* victory, the great victory Jesus won in His death, resurrection, and ascension. We are identified with Him and He with us!

When you read the first two chapters of Paul's letter, you discover that he had gone through difficult experiences in his ministry and was at the point of despairing of life. The sad condition of the church at Corinth was enough to break his heart. Because of his love for them, he had sent them a stern letter of rebuke that he expected them to obey, and this made him feel depressed. The tide of God's blessing seemed at low ebb, but then God began to work matters out. Paul claimed his triumph in Christ and the Lord saw him through. The Lord still does that for His people when situations seem unbearable and our faith is being tested. We are soldiers of Christ (2 Tim. 2:3–4) and our Commander cannot fail.

We Can Always Be "Alive" in Christ (2 Cor. 4:7–18)

Paul now changes the metaphor from soldiers on parade to vessels in God's household. Our bodies, made of clay, are indwelt by the Holy Spirit and contain the treasure of the very life of God. Paul declares a number of wonderful paradoxes in verses 7–12: strength out of weakness, stability in spite of intense pressure, perplexity but not desperation, deliverance to death but always the experience of Christ's abundant life! Because of God's grace and the Holy Spirit's ministry, we die with Christ so that we may live with Christ. (We meet Gal. 2:20 again!) No matter what the circumstances, Paul knew that God would use them to bring glory to Christ, and that was really all that mattered. "For we who live are always delivered to death for Jesus's sake, that the life of Jesus also may be manifested in our mortal flesh" (v. 11). And what is the remarkable result? "So then death is working in us, but life in you" (v. 12).

After molding the vessel, the potter must put it in the furnace to be hardened, otherwise it is useless. It's difficult to find a man or woman in the Bible or in church history whose service for Jesus did not involve some kind of suffering, and that pattern still applies today. If we want to know "the power of His resurrection," we must submit to "the fellowship of His sufferings" (Phil. 3:10). We

THIS IS THE LIFE!

died with Christ that we might manifest the life of Christ (2 Cor. 4:10). My wife and I were privileged to serve three churches and two parachurch ministries, and in all five situations, we had to experience death to self in order to enjoy life in Christ. No pain, no gain—an old adage, but a true one. Jesus called it taking up our cross and following Him. He also compared it to planting a seed in the ground so it might die and bear fruit (John 12:24–26).

We Can Always Be Confident in Christ (2 Cor. 5:6)

Paul was not simply facing difficult times; he was facing death, which is the theme of 2 Corinthians 5:1–8. Death is the ultimate enemy of life, but the eternal life we now have in Jesus Christ cannot die. The human body is pictured here as a tent, and dying is like taking down a tent and leaving it behind so that we can move on to a permanent dwelling in glory. Death for the Christian is not the end of life, it is the beginning of life. In the midst of his troubles, Paul was groaning—but he was groaning for glory! To be at home in the body is to be absent from Christ, but when we leave this mortal body, we are present with Christ. "For we walk by faith, not by sight" (v. 7).

Where do we get this confidence that removes the fear of death and gives us the assurance of heaven? We get it from the Word of God. Let's begin with *the promise that Jesus made.* "I go to prepare a place for you. And if I go and prepare a place for you, I will come again and receive you to Myself, that where I am, there you may be also" (John 14:2–3). If we die before Jesus returns, our spirit goes to heaven to be with Christ. If we are alive when Jesus comes, we will instantly be changed and caught up to go with Him to glory (John 11:25–26; 1 Thess. 4:13–18).

But there is another basis for confidence, and that is *the price that Jesus paid.* We belong to Him, for He purchased us when He died for us on the cross. "For God did not appoint us to wrath,

110

but to obtain salvation through our Lord Jesus Christ, who died for us, that whether we wake or sleep, we should live together with Him" (1 Thess. 5:9–10). A third reason for confidence is *the prayer that Jesus prayed.* "Father, I desire that they also whom you gave Me may be with Me where I am, that they may behold My glory which You have given me" (John 17:24). Jesus prayed that His people might be with Him in heaven! Could the Father refuse to answer the prayer of His beloved Son? Of course not! From joyful hearts, we can praise God for the confidence we have in Christ!

We Can Always Be Sufficient in Christ (2 Cor. 9:6–9)

"Grace giving" is the theme of 2 Corinthians 8 and 9 as Paul encouraged the believers in Corinth to share in the love offering he was collecting for the needy Jewish believers in the holy land. In 9:6–9 he compares the Corinthian Christians to farmers who are planting seed. He points out that there can be no harvest until first the seed has been sown, and the harvest will be in proportion to how much seed was sown. The seed represents the money we give to the Lord for ministry to others, and the entire transaction must be motivated by grace. But our investment in God's people and God's work is backed up by an incredible promise: "And God is able to make all grace abound toward you, that you, always having all sufficiency in all things, may have an abundance for every good work" (2 Cor. 9:8).

Paul begins with "all grace"! There is abundant grace from God, for He is "the God of all grace" (1 Pet. 5:10). The Christian life begins with *saving grace* (Eph. 2:8–9) and continues with *serving grace* (1 Cor. 15:9–10), *sacrificing grace* (2 Cor. 8:1), *suffering grace* (12:1–9), *singing grace* (Col. 3:16), *speaking grace* (4:6), *strengthening grace* (2 Tim. 2:1–4), and *schooling grace* (Titus 2:11–12). Grace is a gift that we receive by faith and God's grace never fails. It is abounding!

Paul continues by assuring us that grace is available "always" no matter what our personal circumstances might be. He experienced the grace of God not only when preaching but also when in prison, during shipwrecks and attacks by mobs, and when funds ran out. I like his phrase "all sufficiency," which covers everything. If we live by grace, then we must be gracious and share with others! In 2 Corinthians 2:16, Paul asked, "And who is sufficient for these things?" The answer is in 3:5, "our sufficiency is from God." No matter what task God sends our way, He will enable us to do it successfully because His grace comes with it. Many times I have found myself saying, "Lord, I can't do this." Then the Lord says, *You're getting like Moses and Jeremiah!* Then I take a deep breath and say, "Sorry, Lord. Please send another shipment of grace." And He always does!

Paul also had his share of sorrowing, but in the end, it was rejoicing in the Lord that triumphed. When I read 2 Corinthians 6:3–10 and discover the trials that Paul experienced, I am amazed that he survived at all. But the same God who cared for Paul is caring for His children today, and He likes to use the word "always." In fact, Jesus used it in His final message to His followers: "And lo, I am with you always, even to the end of the age" (Matt. 28:20).

We Can Always Be Rejoicing in Christ (2 Cor. 6:10)

It's difficult to understand everything about the Christian life, because God's works are beyond human comprehension and "we know in part" (1 Cor. 13:9). However, if we could explain joy in the midst of sorrow and singing in the midst of pain, we would try to achieve it by ourselves—and that would ruin everything. We may not be able to rejoice in our circumstances, but we can always rejoice in our Lord and Savior, knowing that His will comes from His loving heart (Ps. 33:11). With the Spirit's help, we can sing and weep at the same time! There may be pain in the body but there is joy in the heart. "Rejoice in the Lord always. Again I will say, rejoice!" (Phil. 4:4).

Always? That's what Paul wrote—always. If we are praying, living in God's Word, and keeping our eyes and ears open and our heart tender, we will find plenty in life about which we can rejoice, even in the most difficult days. Why not begin with the routine things, the events and people we are prone to take for granted? Satan hates a joyful heart because people who are happy in the Lord don't easily fall into temptation. Why play with the devil's substitutes when we can enjoy "the real thing" from the hand of the Lord?

Our text (2 Cor. 9:8) makes it clear that the reason for our sufficiency in Christ is that we may have "an abundance for every good work." The Lord provides for us so that we may glorify Him as we help to meet the needs of others. Christians are channels, not reservoirs; the best way to conquer covetousness is to praise the Lord and pass the contribution. Until we experience the joy of giving, we will never fully enter into the joy of the Lord.

Whenever I hear unconverted people use the phrase "these poor Christians," I want to shout, "We Christians are the wealthiest people in the world!" And we are, because of the riches of God's grace (Eph. 1:7). "And my God shall supply all your need according to His riches in glory by Christ Jesus" (Phil. 4:19). We are as rich as Jesus is now up in glory, because He shares His riches with us. That's why the Christian life is a life of sufficiency.

12

A Fragrant Life

For we are to God the fragrance of Christ among those who are being saved and among those who are perishing. To the one we are the aroma of death leading to death, and to the other the aroma of life leading to life. And who is sufficient for these things?

2 Corinthians 2:15–16

When I was growing up in northern Indiana, we didn't know much about air pollution, even though we experienced it almost every day. The steel mills, oil refineries, and chemical factories that provided jobs for our community also contributed pollution to the atmosphere. We used to jokingly say, "On a clear day you can see your feet," although it was really not that bad. When the wind changed, the odors in the air also changed, so we always knew which way the wind was blowing.

It is not remarkable that the Bible mentions over a dozen different fragrances, for in the ancient near east perfumed body oils were essential to personal hygiene. Some places did have public baths, but the bath was usually followed by the application of aromatic oils that could smother body odors. The people also burned incense to perfume the air. In the previous chapter about the Roman triumph, we discovered that Christians are bearers of a "spiritual aroma" that says "death" to unbelievers but "life" to those who know Jesus Christ. There should be a special fragrance about God's people that attracts others and gives us opportunities to be a blessing. We have already looked at the fragrance of victory (2 Cor. 2:15–16), but there are other fragrances that ought to be in our lives.

The Fragrance of Prayer (Ps. 141:2)

In the nation of Israel, both the tabernacle and the temple had a small altar that stood before the veil and was used only for burning incense (Exod. 30:1–10, 34–38; 37:25–29). It was made of acacia wood and overlaid with pure gold. Each morning and evening, the high priest would burn special incense on this altar that was used for no other purpose. In Scripture, the burning of incense is a picture of offering prayer to the Lord. David prayed, "Let my prayer be set before You as incense" (Ps. 141:2), and John was told that, in heaven, the prayers of the saints are like incense (Rev. 5:8; 8:1–6). Zacharias the priest was serving at this altar when the angel appeared and announced that he and his wife Elizabeth would have a son, John the Baptist (Luke 1:5–25).

The altar and the incense teach us some important practical truths about prayer. For one thing, our praying must be biblical. God gave Moses the recipe for the incense and made it clear no other incense was permitted, nor was the true incense to be used in any other place. It belonged only on the golden altar before the veil. What are the "ingredients" that make up true prayer? Humility, faith, worship, adoration, the confession of sin, and the claiming of God's promises are certainly essential. The Jewish high priest could go only as far as the veil, but God's people today can enter the holy of holies in heaven and meet the Lord at the throne of grace. How privileged we are!

Just as the priest had specific times each day for this ministry, so we should set aside times daily to meet the Lord in prayer. We should certainly start and close each day with prayer. However, we must also pray during the day as we face different situations. Nehemiah is a great example of "praying without ceasing," and you can find a dozen of his spontaneous prayers recorded in his book. Another essential is the ministry of the Holy Spirit. The incense was burned upon the golden altar, and the Holy Spirit is the "fire" that ignites our prayers. Paul exhorted Timothy to "stir up the gift of God" (2 Tim. 1:6) that was given to him, and that literally means "fan into flame, get the fire going." When the priest came to the golden altar each morning and evening, he first had to remove the cold ashes and rekindle the fire, and so do we need to get rid of the old remnants in our lives and move ahead into the new day or night ahead.

Each time I go to worship or attend a prayer meeting, I am either contributing to the ministry or detracting from it, depending on the spiritual condition of my heart. The priest would not dare to bring "strange fire" into the sanctuary but would get holy fire from the brazen altar where the fire burned continuously. That fire originally came from heaven (Lev. 9:24)! It adds power to a prayer meeting when people attend who habitually pray and, like the Emmaus disciples, have burning hearts (Luke 24:32). The priest chosen to burn the incense would carry away with him from the altar some of the fragrance of the incense, and people could tell that he had been in the sanctuary. Can others detect in us a "holy fragrance" that announces we have been with Jesus?

It's significant that the prayers of God's people are preserved in heaven as incense (Rev. 5:8; 8:3–4). We here on earth may think our stammering prayers are failures, but our Father considers them precious. Our prayers may be despised here on earth, but they are treasured in heaven and bring delight to the Lord. Never underestimate the importance of prayer or the influence of prayer on the people of God and the work of God. The prayer of a little child gets as much attention in heaven as the intercession of an aged prayer warrior.

The Fragrance of Unity (Ps. 133)

Discord and disunity have been problems among God's people ever since Cain killed Abel, Aaron and Miriam criticized their brother Moses, and our Lord's disciples argued over which of them was the greatest. We sing, "We are not divided / All one body we," which is true from God's point of view but not always from the world's point of view. The church in Corinth grieved the Lord and Paul because it was divided four ways (1 Cor. 1:12). I have pastored three churches and ministered in many others, and I have experienced both the godly warmth of unity and the icy blast of disunity. But the imagery in Psalm 133 points the way to a unity that comes from heaven, starting with the word "brethren" in verse 1. That word immediately reminds us that all Christians have experienced a new birth in Christ and belong to the same family. Therefore, we ought to love one another and do all we can to "keep the unity of the Spirit in the bond of peace" (Eph. 4:3).

But I want to focus on the fragrant anointing oil that was used when Aaron was installed as Israel's first high priest. There is a fragrance from personal unity that is absent from organizational uniformity, for unity comes from love within while uniformity results from pressure from without. Inspired by the Holy Spirit, David pointed out that the oil poured on Aaron's head ran down his beard (Ps. 133:2). This meant that the oil bathed the twelve precious stones on Aaron's breastplate, stones that symbolized the twelve tribes of Israel. *The oil united the stones!* This is a picture of the church: "For by one Spirit we were all baptized into one body" (1 Cor. 12:13). No matter where a jewel was set, it was touched by

117

the oil and united with the other stones. Each stone had its own beauty and character, but no one stone was necessarily greater than another. As Aaron bore the tribes over his heart and on his shoulders (Exod. 28), so our Lord Jesus Christ, our heavenly high priest, bears us on His shoulders (with our burdens) and over His heart. At no time does He stop loving us or caring for us!

David, who wrote this psalm, knew something about unity and disunity. When he was young, his own brothers didn't always respect him, and during David's waiting years, Saul divided the nation against him. After Saul's death, David ruled for seven and a half years in Hebron before the entire nation united behind him. Because of envy, lust, and pride, some of David's own sons created disunity in his family and in the nation. True unity is good and pleasant, like the dew that falls on the fields and orchards and produces beauty and fruit (Ps. 133:3). The church doesn't have to manufacture some kind of organizational unity, for we are already one in Christ. Our task is to endeavor "to keep [maintain] the unity of the Spirit in the bond of peace" (Eph. 4:3). If each believer fulfilled that responsibility, then Christ's prayer for unity in John 17 would be answered (vv. 11, 21–23).

The Fragrance of Friendship

"Ointment and perfume delight the heart, and the sweetness of a man's friend gives delight by hearty counsel" (Prov. 27:9). It is a great blessing to have a friend with whom you can discuss important matters, pray, and receive helpful spiritual counsel. That kind of counsel changes the atmosphere of life, just like fragrant perfume changes the atmosphere in a room. To breathe the dull air of depression and disappointment only makes matters worse, but the Lord can use an encouraging friend to bring in a breath of fragrant fresh air.

Our Lord told His disciples that He considered them friends and not servants, "for a servant does not know what his master

is doing" (John 15:13–15). Jesus shares His secrets with us as we
ponder the Word of God, and He proved His friendship by laying
down His life for us. "As iron sharpens iron, so a man sharpens
the countenance of his friend" (Prov. 27:17). I thank the Lord for
the friends who have counseled me, rebuked me, and occasionally
spanked me, because the Lord used their words to put a keener
edge on my ministry. Sometimes their ministry deepened me and
sometimes it convicted me, but it always helped me. Their ministry
carried the fragrance of a garden, not the fire and brimstone of a
battlefield.

When I was a youngster, I had playmates. Then I went to school
and had classmates. In seminary I had a roommate. Then one day
I said "I do" to a life-mate! We have been married more than sixty
years and have had the privilege of ministering in many parts of
the world and meeting many wonderful people. My prayer is that
we have left behind the fragrance of the Lord wherever we have
been, just as others have done for us.

One final thought: the many "one another" statements in the
New Testament remind us that each of us has a responsibility to our
fellow Christians, whether we are strangers, casual acquaintances,
or longtime friends. The "new commandment" that we love one
another is found a dozen times in the Bible, and the other "one
another" statements transform that "love" into specific ministries:
pray for one another (James 5:16), exhort one another (Heb. 3:13),
admonish one another (Rom. 15:14), serve one another (Gal. 5:13),
edify one another (Rom. 14:19), and so on. I think there are more
than twenty of these specific "one another" statements in the Bible
that flesh out the familiar "love one another."

The Fragrance of Sacrifice (Phil. 4:18)

Paul was in prison in Rome. His friends in the church at Philippi
had sent him a special gift of money and supplies that raised his

spirits and met his needs. But Paul didn't see the gift as a church missionary offering. He saw it as "a sweet-smelling aroma, an acceptable sacrifice, well pleasing to God" (Phil. 4:18). By their generous giving, the Philippian saints had delighted the Lord and blessed His servant. Isn't that what giving is all about?

In Scripture, we are frequently told that God "smelled" the sacrifices people offered Him and was pleased with their worship (Gen. 8:21; Lev. 1:9, 13, 17; 26:31). Of course, this is human language used to teach spiritual truth, for God is spirit and does not have a body with a nose for detecting odors. In Scripture, fragrance speaks of acceptance and love while odors speak of judgment and rejection. Some of the plagues the Lord sent to the land of Egypt caused noxious odors (Exod. 7:18, 21; 8:14). Isaiah warned the people that when the day of the Lord came, "instead of a sweet smell there will be a stench" (Isa. 3:24).

I think it was Benjamin Franklin who, as a lad, suggested that his father bless a barrel full of food once-for-all rather than take time to bless it meal by meal, and the boy was disciplined for it. Wise as he was, Franklin missed the point. The table prayer was not just a thanksgiving for the food, it was a sanctifying of the meal, turning it into a special time of fellowship with each other and with the Lord. How many people see their daily meals as "spiritual sacrifices" offered to the Lord and eaten by them like priests in the temple?

In Old Testament days, Jewish believers used to ridicule the Gentiles for worshiping dead idols. "They have mouths, but they do not speak; eyes they have, but they do not see; they have ears, but they do not hear; noses they have, but they do not smell" (Ps. 115:5–6). But our God is alive and aware of the sacrifices we bring to Him because we love Him and want to please Him. *The most important part of a believer's life is the part that only God sees, the private worship and fellowship.* If we truly worship the Lord from our hearts, whatever we lovingly give Him of our time, possessions, and service will be accepted and blessed.

One of the most beautiful examples of this principle is the anointing of Jesus by Mary of Bethany (John 12:1–8). Mary could have used that expensive perfume to prepare her brother Lazarus for burial (John 11), but she saved it for Jesus. Whenever we seek to give our best to Jesus, somebody will criticize us, and that is what Judas did. "Why this waste?" he asked. Imagine calling a gift to Jesus *waste*! Jesus rebuked Judas and said that Mary's worship would be known around the world (Mark 14:9). John tells us that "the house was filled with the fragrance of the oil" (John 12:3). Mary's hair was saturated with the ointment, so wherever she went in the house, she carried the fragrance of worship with her. Cultivating a fragrant life begins at home, but if we are faithful at home the Lord can make us a blessing around the world as He did with Mary! Our private worship will result in public influence on others in ways we know nothing about, and will not know until we get to heaven.

The Fragrance of Forgiveness

When I think of the beautiful fragrance of forgiveness, two Bible characters come to my mind—a famous man in the Old Testament and an anonymous woman in the New Testament, one a king and the other a commoner—both of whom had been involved in sexual sin. But once they had met with the Lord and experienced forgiveness, the result was fragrance.

The man is King David. He committed adultery with Bathsheba and tried to hide his sins, only to experience months of pain and grief (Ps. 32:3–5). After his son was born, the boy became ill and David fasted and prayed that the baby might be spared, but God took his soul to heaven. When he heard the news, "David arose from the ground, washed and anointed himself; and changed his clothes; and he went into the house of the LORD and worshipped" (2 Sam. 12:20).

David took a bath, anointed himself with fragrant perfume, and put on clean clothes. All three actions are used in the Bible in connection with forgiveness. When the Lord forgives us, He washes us, dresses us in clean clothes, and anoints us with the fragrant oil of His blessing. The prodigal son was dressed in the best robe (Luke 15:22). The prophet Zechariah pictures this experience in chapter 3 of his book where he shows the high priest in filthy garments receiving clean garments (vv. 1–5), a picture of God's forgiveness of the sins of the Jewish remnant.

The woman is an anonymous prostitute who heard Jesus preach and give His invitation to sinners, "Come to Me . . . and I will give you rest" (Matt. 11:28–30). She trusted Him and was saved. She must have followed Him to Simon the Pharisee's house, where Jesus was dining, and there she washed His feet with her tears, wiped them with her hair, and anointed His feet with choice oils (Luke 7:36–50). The perfume she once used for evil was now given to her Savior, and He accepted it. It was the fragrance of forgiveness. Jesus pronounced her forgiven, and this shocked Simon but comforted the woman. Then Jesus said, "Your faith has saved you. Go in peace," and the matter was settled (v. 50).

Those whom God has forgiven, we must forgive. Simon had not yet learned that lesson. Sin has put a great deal of pollution into the atmosphere of this world, and God's people are the only ones who can make a difference. Are we radiating the fragrance of forgiveness in our homes, churches, friendships, and places of employment?

13

A Quiet and Peaceable Life

Aspire to lead a quiet life, to mind your own business, and to work with your own hands, as we commanded you.

1 Thessalonians 4:11

That we may lead a quiet and peaceable life in all godliness and reverence.

1 Timothy 2:2

Modern life seems always competitive, even to getting the last parking place at the supermarket. Modern life is complex as I try to figure out the latest edition of the device I use to test my blood sugar. Modern life is also extremely noisy. I'm sitting quietly on the patio, wanting to read a book, and three neighbors decide to mow their lawns, another neighbor turns up the volume on his radio as he washes his wife's car, and a vehicle with a broken muffler goes coughing down the street. A few moments later a teen drives by with a boom box, telling everybody that he has bad taste in music and a bad future for his hearing. I finally retreat into the house, put some quiet music on the stereo, and enjoy reading my book.

But I'm smart enough to know that it isn't the noise on the outside that distracts me, but the noise *on the inside*. Counselors tell us that we have a chorus of voices within us that compliment us, criticize us, correct us, sometimes confuse us, and always try to control us, and that's why we lose our peace. One voice shouts, *You have a book to write!* Another one whispers, *The mail needs to be answered.* A third one reminds me that there are stacks of newspapers, aluminum cans, and plastic bottles to be taken to the recycle bins. In my ministry I have flown thousands of miles, and I know that planes and airports are noisy, but on almost every trip I always completed my work. The secret of a quiet and peaceful life is not perfect silence in perfect isolation but a quiet mind and a quiet heart under the control of the Spirit of God. "You will keep him in perfect peace, whose mind is stayed on You, because he trusts in You" (Isa. 26:3).

How does our loving Father help His children to live quiet and peaceable lives in a world that is so noisy and competitive? Here are some of the ministries He wants to share with us, if we will let Him.

He Leads Us

"He makes me to lie down in green pastures; He leads me beside the still waters" (Ps. 23:2). The pasture provides food and the stream provides water, but there is more here than physical sustenance. Sheep need to lie down and rest, and sheep are afraid of rapidly moving water. If the flock is to be ready for the next stage of the journey, it must be allowed to enjoy peaceful rest. Jesus said to His disciples, "Come aside by yourselves to a deserted place and rest a while" (Mark 6:31). Vance Havner used to say, "If you don't come apart and rest, you will come apart!" An energetic pastor friend of mine was in the hospital for emergency surgery and my wife and I went to visit him. "I have so much work to do," he said, and I replied, "But the Scripture says, 'He makes me to lie down.'" He took a deep breath and replied, "I tell that to other people."

Sometimes the Lord has to set us aside so we can catch up on the past. We get so involved with new ideas and new gadgets and new challenges that we need a week in bed to think back and learn from the old times. Jeremiah told the confused Jewish people, "Stand in the ways and see, and ask for the old paths, where the good way is, and walk in it; then you will find rest for your souls" (Jer. 6:16). One evening as I was driving home, a drunk driver hit me going eighty miles an hour, and I was set aside for about three months, two weeks of that time in the hospital. For a week I lived on ice, fruit juice, and cottage cheese. When the aide brought me my first real meal, I was ecstatic. Food never tasted so good! (I learned later that the meal I ate belonged to another patient, but it was too late for the aide to do anything about it.) Occasionally we need to "come apart" and rest and discover how wonderful family and friends are, how good food is, how tired our bodies are, how precious time and life are, how nice most people are, and what a privilege it is to be alive and serving Jesus.

He Disciplines Us

My father had the fastest belt in Indiana. I didn't enjoy being disciplined, but I profited from it. When I was in my teens and had become a Christian, Hebrews 12 became a meaningful chapter to me and it still is. "Now no chastening seems to be joyful for the present, but grievous; nevertheless, afterward it yields the peaceable fruit of righteousness to those who have been trained by it" (Heb. 12:11). I especially like the New Living Translation version of the phrase "the peaceable fruit of righteousness"—"a peaceful harvest of right living." The Lord has more than once said to me what He said to Peter, "What I am doing you do not understand now, but you will know after this" (John 13:7).

Following every discipline experience, the Lord gives us "a peaceful harvest" to enjoy. After a parent disciplines a child, the tears will be wiped away, and there will be hugs and kisses and perhaps even a special treat. As young as I was, I rejoiced when the spanking was over; I was forgiven and my family still loved me. The prophet Zephaniah expresses this beautifully: "The Lord your God is with you, the Mighty Warrior who saves. He will take great delight in you; in his love he will no longer rebuke you, but will rejoice over you with singing" (Zeph. 3:17 NIV). I see God the Father picking up His fretful child and holding the child close to His heart while He sings a lovely song. Yes, God sings! This is part of the "quiet harvest" that follows loving discipline.

He Weans Us (Ps. 131)

Jewish children were weaned between ages three and four, so they were old enough to protest being taken from their mother's arms where her exclusive love was so delightful. But it was time for the children to start growing up, feeding themselves and helping their mother with some of the household chores. The child that is not weaned is in bondage, unable to enjoy the freedoms that every child deserves. To be a "mama's baby" all your life is not the secret of a productive happy life!

The Lord's goal for each of His children is maturity. Growing old is a given; growing up is a choice, and we make the decision. To stay in the primary department of the Sunday School because you receive treats is a poor motive for standing still in your Bible study and refusing to discuss the Scriptures with your peers. There is always more to learn and to do, and the process is called *maturing*.

As we mature spiritually, we learn to cultivate a quiet heart. Things I used to fuss over early in my Christian walk no longer enter my

.mind, and as I look back I wonder why I was disturbed in the first place. Sometimes the Lord has to wean us away from things we enjoy that are keeping us from growing up. Abraham and Sarah had to give up their home and family in Ur, and one day, Abraham had to give up his son Isaac! Joseph had to give up father, family, and home before the Lord could equip him to be second ruler of Egypt so he could rescue his family. It isn't only bad things that God takes from us, for even good things can hinder our maturing if they become idols.

The key is *submission*. The child who submits to mother's will discovers a whole new world of enrichment *and the child has been set free to enjoy it*! Paul says it perfectly: "when I became a man, I put away childish things" (1 Cor. 13:11). I have seen churches crippled and almost destroyed by people who will not give up their toys. If clothing revealed spiritual stature, they would have been wearing diapers. In Psalm 131, David tells the Lord he's through being upset like a child and is now "calmed and quieted."

Am I in need of weaning? Is there anything in my life that is childish and needs to be removed? If I desire a quiet and peaceable life, I had better give my toys to Jesus and let Him lead me into maturity and victory.

He Yokes Us to Jesus

One of the greatest invitations Jesus ever gave is recorded in Matthew, and it holds one of the keys of a quiet and peaceful heart.

> Come to Me, all you who labor and are heavy laden, and I will give you rest. Take My yoke upon you and learn from Me, for I am gentle and lowly in heart, and you will find rest for your souls. For My yoke is easy and My burden is light. (Matt. 11:28–30)

The first step the restless sinner must take is to come to Jesus and receive the gift of salvation, which includes the gift of rest. "Therefore, having been justified by faith, we have peace with God

THIS IS THE LIFE!

through our Lord Jesus Christ" (Rom. 5:1). But that is only the beginning. We must take Christ's yoke and yield ourselves wholly to Him so that we are yoked together in doing the will of God. To the farmer in New Testament times, taking the yoke meant completely controlling an animal that had been broken, and to a student it meant submitting completely to a rabbi and listening and learning.

Everybody is "yoked" to something—property, money, other people, sins, religious rituals—but these yokes have a way of running our lives and do not bring freedom. British theologian Peter T. Forsythe said, "The purpose of life is not to find your freedom but to find your master." How do you become a great athlete? By putting yourself under the mastery of a great coach. Do you want to be a great musician? Then surrender to a great musician and learn. Do you want to live a great life? Then submit to the greatest Life of all—Jesus Christ, the Son of God.

Come—take—learn. This means spending time in the Word of God and with the people of God, learning all we can about the Son of God and putting it into practice. "Come" is a crisis and so is "take," but "learn" is a process that goes on and on. Jesus is not telling us simply to learn about the Bible but to learn about Him from the Bible. The Holy Spirit desires to show us Jesus in the Scriptures and to help us to love Him more and serve Him better.

Come—take—learn—find. The peace we have when we come to Jesus is peace *with* God, for we are now His children and not His enemies. But the peace we find as we grow spiritually is the peace of God!

> Be anxious for nothing, but in everything by prayer and supplication, with thanksgiving, let your requests be made known to God; and the peace of God, which surpasses all understanding, will guard your hearts and minds through Christ Jesus. (Phil. 4:6–7)

This is the rest we find as we "grow in the grace and knowledge of our Lord and Savior Jesus Christ" (2 Pet. 3:18).

So, if you want to experience a quiet and peaceable life, get yoked to Jesus and learn! Jesus said, "These things have I spoken to you, that in Me you may have peace" (John 16:33). The better we know Him and His Word, the more we will enjoy His peace.

He Encourages Us to Pray

"If it is possible, as much as depends on you, live peaceably with all men" (Rom. 12:18).

> Therefore I exhort first of all that supplications, prayers, intercessions, and giving of thanks be made for all men, for kings and all who are in authority, that we may lead a quiet and peaceable life in all godliness and reverence. For this is good and acceptable in the sight of God our Savior. (1 Tim. 2:1–3)

Granted, there are situations over which we have no control, but we can pray and ask God to work. Some people are like sandpaper and the Lord uses them to polish us, while others are professional critics and complainers who constantly test our patience. I have learned to pray for these people who make life difficult, and the Lord has worked in me and in them and helped us both. Let's be sure we are the victims and not the offenders!

Believing prayer solves problems. There is a peace that comes to the heart when you commit everything to the Lord and trust Him to work. I recall one serious church problem that required five years of faith and patience as we prayed and waited, but the problem was solved!

He Teaches Us the Scriptures

"These things I have spoken to you, that in Me you may have peace. In the world you will have tribulation; but be of good cheer, I have overcome the world" (John 16:33). While in the upper room with

His disciples (John 13–16), Jesus explained many important spiritual truths that they would need to grasp and apply after He had returned to heaven. If we turn to the Word of God only in times of trouble, we are robbing ourselves, but if we meditate on the Scriptures daily, we will be fortified in faith and able to confront the enemy. "Great peace have those who love Your law, and nothing causes them to stumble" (Ps. 119:165).

Jesus told His disciples, "Peace I leave with you, My peace I give to you; not as the world gives do I give to you. Let not your heart be troubled, neither let it be afraid" (John 14:27). How does the world give peace? Either by sedation or distraction. You can go to the pharmacy and purchase pills that will calm you down, but they will not build you up so you can face and solve your problems. Or you can go to a baseball game, a movie, or on a shopping spree, and forget all about it for two or three hours, but the problem will still be there. Through the Word of God and the Holy Spirit, Jesus gives us what we need to face and solve our problems in His time and in His way. Every Christian needs a list of Scripture texts that have in the past brought help in times of testing. Better yet, memorize these key verses and have them ready when the enemy attacks. That's the way Jesus defeated Satan in the wilderness, and it will work for you.

He Gives Us Work to Do

Yes, He makes us to lie down (Ps. 23:2), and there are times when a good nap helps solve problems. But He also helps us to get up and go to work! But how can work contribute to a quiet life? To do the work the Lord has assigned to us is a privilege, not a punishment. Even before sin entered the scene, our first parents had work to do in the garden. Have you noticed in Scripture that many of the people God called into His service were busy at work when He called them? Moses was caring for sheep, Gideon was threshing wheat, David was tending his father's flock, Peter, Andrew, James, and John were mending nets, and Matthew was collecting taxes. Before He began His ministry, our Lord Jesus Christ was a carpenter (Mark 6:3), and Paul was a tentmaker throughout his years of service.

There is no place in God's kingdom for lazy people, particularly lazy pastors. For the dedicated Christian, every legitimate work is service for the Lord, and to waste time is to sin. As much "divine service" is done by a mother in the kitchen and laundry as by a preacher in the pulpit or a missionary translating the Bible. The dignity of work done well honors the Lord. Work done from the heart to God's glory is a form of worship. Even when we have tired bodies and minds, if we have done our work well, there is a joy in our hearts that only God can give. "The sleep of a laboring man is sweet" (Eccles. 5:12). "The work of righteousness will be peace, and the effect of righteousness, quietness and assurance forever" (Isa. 32:17).

Paul had a problem in the church at Thessalonica: some of the members were quitting their jobs and lounging around waiting for the return of the Lord (2 Thess. 3:6–15). They were wrong, of course, because the Lord wants to find us busy and faithful when He returns (Mark 13:32–37). Having done a good day's work makes a person feel good in spite of weariness of the body and mind. There is a God-given satisfaction in work well done, "for it is God who works in you both to will and to do for His good pleasure" (Phil. 2:13).

14

A Life of Freedom

If you abide in My word, you are My disciples indeed. And you shall know the truth, and the truth shall make you free.

John 8:31–32

God's purpose for His people and His creation is *freedom*, what Paul calls "the glorious liberty of the children of God" (Rom. 8:21). The day will come when God's people will have glorified bodies and live in a wonderful new environment, free from the forms of bondage that we endure in this life. But even today we may experience the freedom Christ gives us, for "if the Son makes you free, you shall be free indeed" (John 8:36).

But first we must consider the question, "What is freedom?" The usual answer is, "Freedom means being able to do whatever you want to do, or not do what you don't want to do"—an answer that is wickedly wrong. Doing whatever you want to do or not doing what you don't want to do is actually the worst kind of bondage and selfishness, and ultimately leads to the lowest kind of existence.

Here is my definition of freedom: "Freedom is life controlled by truth and motivated by love, leading to ministry and maturity." Pause and give that definition some thought.

Freedom Is Life . . .

Corpses, marble statues, and skeletons have no freedom because they have no life. I admired the artistry in Madame Tussaud's Waxworks on Marylebone Road in London, but none of the wax statues spoke to me or offered to shake my hand. Unsaved people have no true freedom because they are "dead in trespasses and sins" (Eph. 2:1). Unsaved people may even be religious, but God calls their religion "dead works" because the people practicing them are spiritually dead (Heb. 6:1; 9:14). When Jesus raised Lazarus from the dead, He commanded, "Loose him, and let him go" (John 11:44), and they removed the malodorous grave clothes and dressed him as a living man, which he now was.

Millions of people are miserable because they have things backward. As we saw in chapter 1, eternal life is a gift that can be received only by trusting Jesus Christ. "He who believes in the Son has everlasting life, and he who does not believe the Son shall not see life, but the wrath of God abides on him" (John 3:36)—present tense, *right now!* British theologian P. T. Forsyth said it right: "The first duty of every soul is to find not its freedom but its Master."[1]

If you want to be a great athlete, you put yourself under the authority of a great coach, trust him or her, and do what they command. Great musicians, artists, writers, and leaders are made the same way: find the right master and follow. The greatest Master of all is Jesus Christ, and freedom begins with submission to Him.

1. P. T. Forsyth, *Positive Preaching and Modern Mind* (New York: Eaton & Mains, 1907), 28.

Freedom Is Life Controlled by Truth . . .

Life must be controlled by truth, for if it is controlled by doubts or lies, the consequences will be painful. Jesus is truth (John 14:6), the Holy Spirit is truth (1 John 5:6), the Scriptures are truth (John 17:17), and the church is "the pillar and ground of the truth" (1 Tim. 3:15). If we allow the Spirit to teach us about Jesus from the Scriptures, and if we fellowship in love with the people of God, the truth will become a living part of us and we will walk in truth (2 John 4). God's truth will not just *inform* us but it will also *transform* us so that we become more and more like Jesus Christ.

Many of today's so-called intellectuals deny that there is such a thing as truth. "What is truth for you may not be truth for me," they protest. But Moses, the prophets, Jesus, and His apostles all affirmed that God has given us His truth; and the personal experience of faithful believers down through the centuries has affirmed it. Sir Winston Churchill said, "Truth is incontrovertible. Panic may resent it; ignorance may deride it; malice may distort it; but there it is!" Indeed, there it is! "Forever, O LORD, Your word is settled in heaven" (Ps. 119:89).

When it comes to measurements, even the unbelieving "intellectuals" accept them as absolutes: feet and inches, meters and millimeters, pints and gallons, feet and miles, pounds and ounces. Without these standards, we would be living in costly confusion. Whether an astronomer is gazing through a telescope at a vast galaxy or an oncologist is peering through a microscope at a tiny blood sample, both are depending on absolutes. Episcopal bishop Phillips Brooks said, "Truth is always strong, no matter how weak it looks, and falsehood is always weak, no matter how strong it looks."

There is a false freedom that depends on lies and leads to disaster and defeat. The apostle Peter warns us against false teachers who infiltrate churches and schools and introduce ideas that are contrary to the inspired Word of God (2 Peter 2). During more than sixty years of ministry, I have seen various ministries get infected with false doctrines, divide, weaken, and then die. Paul compared false doctrine to yeast: let a small amount get into the dough and it will spread and infect the whole lump (Luke 12:1; Gal. 5:9; 1 Cor. 5:6–8).

Freedom Is Life Controlled by Truth and Motivated by Love . . .

Wherever you find an angry person, filled with hatred, malice, and a desire for revenge, you will find a person about to go out of control and destroy that which is precious. Someone has said that anger is like an acid that does more harm to the vessel in which it is stored than to the person on whom it is poured. American humorist Will Rogers warned us that people who fly into a rage usually make a bad landing. "Cease from anger, and forsake wrath; do not fret—it only causes harm" (Ps. 37:8).

"But the fruit of the Spirit is love" (Gal. 5:22). I used to tell my ministerial students that 1 Corinthians 13 was not written to be read at weddings or funerals but *at church board meetings and congregational business meetings.* There are many people who get angry when they can't have their own way, and some of them are church members. If our hearts are filled with love from the Spirit, then we will be able to obey James 1:19–20. "Let every man be swift to hear, slow to speak, slow to wrath; for the wrath of man does not produce the righteousness of God." Unrighteous anger is a vicious weapon from the devil, and we all need the self-control that is motivated by love.

Christian love is not something that we manufacture ourselves. It is fruit that grows from our hearts as we humble ourselves, meditate on the Scriptures, pray for God's help, and walk in the Spirit day by day. We will be tested by what people say and do, and we will be tempted to get angry; but that's when we must look to the Lord for "the peace of God, which surpasses all understanding" (Phil. 4:5–7). If we find ourselves being tempted by the same people, we must examine our hearts to see if there is something there that the Lord wants removed. We cannot have freedom from anger until we are controlled by truth, and it's very easy for us to lie to ourselves! Meditate on 1 John 1:5–10 and Psalm 139:23–24.

Of course, our love for others is an outflow of our love for the Lord. To the Christian believer, loving others means treating them the way God treats us. Paul's prayer for his friends in Philippi is a good example for us to follow.

> And this I pray, that your love may abound still more and more in knowledge and all discernment, that you may approve the things that are excellent, that you may be sincere and without offense till the day of Christ, being filled with the fruits of righteousness which are by Jesus Christ, to the glory and praise of God. (Phil. 1:9–11)

Christian love is not only to abound in fullness in our lives, but it should also be to grow in knowledge and discernment. Romantic love may be blind, but Christian love is *not* blind. We love with our eyes wide open! We must distinguish the things that differ, for love and truth go together (Eph. 4:15). Love without truth is hypocrisy and truth without love is brutality, and we must be balanced.

Whenever we serve others, we do so not only because we love them but also because we love Jesus. Paul calls this "the affection of Jesus Christ" (Phil. 1:8). "Assuredly, I say unto you," said Jesus, "inasmuch as you did it to one of the least of these My brethren, you did it to Me" (Matt. 25:40). Whenever we help Christians, we must remember that Christ dwells in them; and whenever we help unsaved people, we must remember that Christ loves them and died for them. Christ must be at the heart of our loving. Furthermore, whatever service we render must bring glory to the Lord because we want Christ to be magnified (Phil. 1:20). The microscope makes small things large and the telescope makes distant things near. Most lost people think Jesus is very small—not as important as their favorite athlete or TV star—and very far away, but when we magnify Christ in serving others, Jesus becomes big and near!

Freedom Is Life Controlled by Truth and Motivated by Love, Leading to Ministry and Maturity

We are not truly free until we put Jesus first, others next, and ourselves last. If we are not careful, even our Christian ministry can be used to glorify ourselves instead of glorifying our Father in heaven (Matt. 5:16). If people see only us but not Jesus, we have failed. If God's servants deserve it, there is a time and place for the Lord to honor faithful service (1 Thess. 5:12–13), but we must not be constantly promoting ourselves. While driving to minister at a conference, I was listening to a preacher on a Christian radio station, but finally turned him off. He was saying very little about Jesus and very much about himself. He had forgotten the concern of John the Baptist: "He must increase, but I must decrease" (John 3:30).

Our freedom in Christ must lead to ministry that glorifies Christ. Peter tells us that we must not use our liberty as a cloak for sin, but to serve the Lord (1 Pet. 2:16). If ministry does not help produce spiritual maturity in the servant, something is wrong. Nature has determined that we grow old, but our own decisions and goals determine whether we grow up. Maturing servants of God have several characteristics, the first of which is *they know themselves and accept themselves.* I have had to serve with Christians who were living on illusions and not reality. They thought they had certain gifts, but they didn't, and this error created serious problems. I learned very early in life that I had no athletic, artistic, or technical ability, but that I was a good student, a fast reader, a patient listener, and a capable speaker. I focused on my strengths, learned to live with my weaknesses—a sense of humor helps—and by the grace of God managed to find God's will for my life.

Maturing people improve themselves. They don't settle for a comfortable, easy place in life but accept challenges and keep growing. I knew a man who, when he was in grade school, deliberately failed the third grade because he didn't want to go to the fourth grade and have to write with ink! I wonder how he would have handled computers! I like the attitude of Caleb: "Now therefore, give me this mountain" (Josh. 14:12). Each task we accept prepares us for the next one, if we are willing to pay the price of moving on. Give me this mountain!

With the help of the Lord, maturing people *discipline themselves*. They submit to authority and stick to the assignment until it's finished. They avoid costly shortcuts and refuse to make excuses. (Evangelist Billy Sunday said that an excuse was the skin of a reason stuffed with a lie.) The worker who one day wants to give orders must first learn to take orders. That was our Lord's philosophy of work: "Well done, good and faithful servant; you were faithful over a few things, I will make you ruler over many things. Enter into the joy of your lord" (Matt. 25:21). Disciplined workers go from few things to many things, from servants to rulers and from toil to joy—if they are faithful.

In short, the maturing servant becomes more and more like Jesus Christ. During His earthly ministry, He was a faithful servant, approved by the Father and filled with the Spirit. He loved those to whom He ministered. He willingly suffered, sacrificed, and died. In every way, He is the perfect example of servant, leader, and victor. As our high priest in heaven, He ministers to us, in us, and through us that He might perfect us in character and make us effective in ministry.

While working my way through the Epistle to the Hebrews, I noticed three parallel verses that taught me an important lesson about spiritual maturity: under the old covenant, the priests made nothing perfect (7:11), the law made nothing perfect (v. 19), and the sacrifices made nothing perfect (10:1). No matter how helpful preachers, teachers, and spiritual leaders may be, only Jesus can keep us in the will of God and produce maturity. No matter how many disciplines or systems of religious rules we may adopt and try to follow, they will not change us, for only the Holy Spirit can do that (2 Cor. 3:18). No matter how much we willingly sacrifice and suffer, only the grace of God can make us more like Jesus. We are not transformed by saying so many prayers, or giving so much money, or obeying so many rules, but by coming to our great High Priest at His throne of grace and worshiping Him so He can meet our needs and give us the grace that only He can bestow. The life that is free depends not on the things of this earth but on the glorious resources of heaven, what Paul called "His riches in glory in Christ Jesus" (Phil. 4:19).

> Because we willingly give ourselves to Jesus Christ and obey Him, we are free.
>
> Because we believe God's truth and obey it, we are free.
>
> Because we love Christ and share that love with others, we are free.
>
> Because the Spirit enlightens and empowers us, we are free.
>
> "Stand fast therefore in the liberty by which Christ has made us free" (Gal. 5:1).

15

Saints Alive!

For to me, to live is Christ.

Philippians 1:21

When I was a child, the combination of the Depression and three older siblings challenged me to use my imagination when I wanted to play. We had the basic toys, of course, but being the baby of the family, I was frequently last in line. I'm grateful for this, however, because I really had to use my imagination *and I am still using it!* My sister and I played "school," complete with roll calls, assignments, tests, and grades. She also enjoyed playing "house" and "store," but whenever she did, that was my signal to round up the boys in the neighborhood and get busy in a game of "cops and robbers" or "cowboys and Indians."

Children play at life and benefit from it, but Christian adults can't afford that luxury. Life is real, life is demanding, and life is serious; one day we will answer to the Lord for the way we used our time on earth. God put us here, not to play at life *but to live!*

The foolish and the lazy may waste their lives, but not the dedicated Christian. American psychologist and philosopher William James wrote, "The great use of life is to spend it for something that outlasts it." Substitute the word *invest* for *spend* and you have the Christian point of view. We are investing our lives in the kingdom of God! Is there any greater privilege than that?

As we have walked together through this book, we have examined several aspects of the Christian life. But the Christian life isn't something we analyze and explain; it's something we live and experience and share day by day. It's a privilege to be a Christian believer. Each day that the Lord gives us is an opportunity to glorify Him as we minister to others. I trust that the truths I have shared have encouraged you to join Paul in saying, "For to me, to live is Christ."

If you are hesitating in this matter of committing your life to serving Jesus Christ, where you are now or wherever He sends you, please prayerfully consider the following statements.

There Are No Unimportant People in God's Family

You may think that you don't qualify as a servant of the Lord, but the Lord thinks otherwise. Not every man is a Moses, a Gideon, a David, or a Paul, and not every woman is a Sarah, a Rachel, a Deborah, or a Mary. God addressed Gideon as "a mighty man of valor" before Gideon ever fought a battle (Judg. 6:12), and He told Simon he was a rock (Peter) before he began to follow Him (John 1:40–42). You are important to the Lord and He can equip you to be all that He wants you to be and to do all that He wants you to do.

There Are No Insignificant Places

Often in my conference ministry, I have been approached by people who open the conversation with, "I'm pastoring a small church"—and I interrupt them with, "Excuse me, there are no small churches and there are no big preachers. How can I help you?" Especially in the United States, believers are mired in the Book of Numbers and forget God's question in Zechariah 4:10, "For who has despised the day of small things?" No matter what the statistics might be, every place is an important place if God's people are serving faithfully and seeking to glorify Jesus Christ.

There Are No Insoluble Problems

God doesn't call losers. Their unbelief might make them losers, but that wasn't God's original plan. Moses did his best to beg off, but the Lord made a mighty leader out of him. Gideon and Jeremiah had a list of reasons why they would fail, but they succeeded. All of us have handicaps of one kind or another, but the Lord can solve every problem and turn weakness into strength and seeming defeat into victory. Problem people in the church? Opposition from government officials? A desperate need for workers and finances? God has not changed since He told Peter to write "[cast] all your care upon Him, for He cares for you" (1 Pet. 5:7); and Philippians 4:13 and 4:19 are still valid. Unbelief sees obstacles, but faith sees opportunities.

There Are No Alternatives

To try to negotiate the will of God means losing the best that God has planned for us, because He always gives His best to those who leave the choices with Him. The parable of the workers in the vineyard makes this very clear (Matt. 20:1–16). The workers who insisted on a contract were paid exactly what they asked for, while the workers who trusted the foreman received far more than they deserved. To attempt to negotiate the will of God means we think we know more than God knows, and it's also an evidence of unbelief. Since God's will comes from God's loving heart (Ps. 33:11), we have nothing to fear. Let the Lord write the contract. Better yet, forget the contract and simply trust Him.

There Is No Greater Privilege

As ambassadors of Jesus Christ, we serve a gracious and generous King who never forsakes us and always provides for us. We have the Scriptures to guide us, the Holy Spirit to teach us and empower us, and the throne of grace available to us to meet our every need. We follow in the train of some of the most wonderful men and women who ever lived, and we help to meet the greatest need in a world that desperately needs forgiveness, peace, and the assurance of heaven. To carry the message of the gospel to a hopeless people is a privilege we don't deserve and we dare not ignore.

We are saints alive! We have eternal life and all its privileges, and we can share the message of life with others. "Behold, now is the accepted time; behold, now is the day of salvation" (2 Cor. 6:2).

Warren W. Wiersbe has served as a pastor, radio Bible teacher, and seminary instructor and is the author or editor of more than 160 books, including the popular BE series of Bible expositions. He pastored the Moody Church in Chicago and also ministered with Back to the Bible Broadcast for ten years, five of them as Bible teacher and general director. His conference ministry has taken him to many countries. He and his wife, Betty, make their home in Nebraska, where he continues his writing ministry.